CHALK HILL
2003 ESTATE BOTTLED
SAUVIGNON BLANC
CHALK HILL APPELLATION
RUSSIAN RIVER VALLEY
Frederick and Peggy Furth, Proprietors

MILLE e una NOTT

DONNAFUGATA

GLASS MOUNTAIN®
by MARKHAM®
2002
SYRAH
CALIFORNIA
VINTNER'S SELECTION

PINOT GRIGIO
CHARDONNAY
VARIETALS
2004
PASQUA

LENTON BRAE
MARGARET RIVER
2002
CABERNET SAUVIGNON

»ZIEREC
SAUVIGN
BLAN
TEMEL
BERGHAUS

53 - 2003

2003
Château
outon Rothschild

WHITE
ZINFANDEL
MENDOCINO COUNTY
ALC. 12.5% BY VOL.

PEDRONCELLI
SONOMA COUNTY
PINOT NOIR
RUSSIAN RIVER VALLEY
2004
Sonoma County

2003
RIESLING
INNERE BERGEN

SEGÚ

RESERVE
Carménère

CHANTELEURS

CHAMPAGNE
HENRIOT
MAISON FONDEE EN 1808
1990
BRUT

Lackner-Tinnacher

2003
Sauvignon blanc
Südsteiermark

T

IEREGG«
UVIGNON
BLANC
EMENT
ERGHAUSEN

2001
MARKHAM
VINEYARDS®
Petite Sirah
NAPA VALLEY
ALC. 14.2% BY VOL.

BAROSSA
SHIRAZ & VIOGNIER
14.0% alc./vol.   RED WINE 2004 VIN ROUGE   750ML
PRODUCT OF AUSTRALIA PRODUIT D'AUSTRALIE
BOTTLED BY | MIS EN BOUTEILLE PAR YALUMBA EDEN VALLEY RD ANGASTON S.A. 5353

JOSEPH PHELPS
VINEYARDS
MISTRAL
2002
MONTEREY COUNTY
RED WINE

2004
PINOT GRIGIO
VENEZIE

Barbera d'Asti
Denominazione di origine
controllata
2003
piccosul capoche.com

Imbottigliato da
"Braida"

Grand Vin de Bourgogne
CHARMES - CHAMBERTIN
GRAND CRU
Appellation Contrôlée
PRODUCT OF FRANCE
Mis en bouteille par MOILLARD®   750

Wine with Asian Food

Wine with Asian Food

NEW FRONTIERS IN TASTE

Patricia Guy & Edwin Soon

TIDE-MARK PRESS, LTD.

PREFACE

Our quest to discover a systematic method for matching wines with Asian food began as a simple exchange of correspondence. We both kept coming across the notion that Sauvignon Blanc made an ideal partner for Thai food, an idea with which neither of us agreed. We felt that a less herbaceous wine was called for and settled on the floral and slightly mineral notes of a top-flight Soave. Every snippet of wine pairing lore that struck us as inappropriate inspired a fresh volley of e-mails. From hypothetical musings we began to test our theories – in Singapore, Verona, and points in between.

We dined at Tan Dinh in Paris, where we matched fine Burgundian wines with Vietnamese cuisine. At Tabla's in New York we sampled Indian flavors – cumin, curry, and coriander – with demi-sec Vouvray. At Norman's in Los Angeles we found that an Austrian Grüner Veltliner and an off-dry Scheurebe from Rheinhessen both worked well with a delicious, vegetable-filled Vietnamese spring roll. We matched wines with New Wave Japanese dishes at Kahala in Osaka and at the Armani Nobu in Milan. At The Chairman and Yip in Canberra, and Hua Ting in Singapore, we sampled Chinese food, each course served with a selection of different wines.

We became aware that restaurants offering Asian flavors were now well established around the world and were also earning top marks for their wine selections. Just as the popularity of Asian restaurants in Western countries had been increasing, an analogous phenomenon was taking place in the East – namely, the growing understanding and enjoyment of fine wine. Another of our gastronomic forays, for example, took us to the rather simple and rustic Sin Huat Eating House in Geylang, which is the red light district of Singapore, where customers are encouraged to bring their own wine. We did, and to our pleasant surprise, the proprietor even supplied stemmed glasses and a corkscrew.

We began, therefore, to examine the characteristics of wine (tannin, acidity, sweetness, and fruitiness) and their interaction with specific Asian flavors and cooking techniques, such as the exquisite balance of sweet and sour flavors, the nutty smokiness that comes from stir frying, and the dark richness of a soy sauce glaze.

The more we cooked, read, tasted, and tried different combinations, the more we came to realize that the definitive work on the pairing of wine with Asian flavors had yet to be written. And so our book was born. It is the result of our successful trials, like those touched on above, as well as our errors. Most important, though, we are thrilled to have the opportunity to share with you those matches that worked. Some of them are truly celestial marriages, others are simply very good liaisons.

We have distilled our experience into an uncomplicated method, one that will allow you to make effortless yet informed decisions when selecting a wine to accompany your Asian meals, whether at a restaurant or at home. Our aim is to give you the guidelines and the confidence to explore your own tastes and, indeed, try out dishes and wines that we do not specifically mention. There is a real joy in combining wine with Asian food. The process gives you the chance to explore new aromas and flavors, both in the dish and in the glass.

We wrote this book out of our common love of cooking and our shared passion for wine, developed over some twenty years of working with this fascinating product. We are delighted to share our experience with you and hope that this book will guide you on a journey toward exciting new taste sensations.

Published by Tide-mark Press, Ltd.
P.O. Box 20, Windsor, CT 06095
In Canada: 34 Armstrong Avenue, Georgetown, Ontario L7G 4R9

Text copyright 2007 by Patricia Guy and Edwin Soon
Recipes copyright 2007 by Edwin Soon
Food photographs copyright 2007 by Ee Kay Gie

Library of Congress Control Number 2006934272
ISBN 978-1-59490-114-7

Printed in Singapore

TIDE-MARK
www.tidemarkpress.com

CONTENTS

Matching Wine and Asian Food

Do wines go with Asian food? Certainly! In Asia, diners are already enjoying wines with their meals, and in the West, it is not uncommon to see authentic Asian restaurants proffering wine lists.

With Western food, the choice of wine is not too difficult. You already know the three basic rules: Red wine is an ideal match for red meat, while white wine makes a good foil for fish and poultry. If you are serving a regional speciality from a wine-producing zone, it is best to choose the wine that evolved alongside the dish – Sancerre with goat's cheese, Riesling with sauerkraut and bratwurst, and Spanish Rosado with paella.

In the case of Asian food, finding suitable wine matches can become complicated. Typically at an Asian meal, several dishes are served at the same time and are shared by everyone present. The wine chosen for such a meal has to be versatile.

The other difficulty arises from the flavors of Asian dishes. Most of them, whatever the "main ingredient" may be, are prepared in such a way that it is not the meat, seafood, or vegetables that stand out as the predominant flavor. Rather, the true flavor of the dish may be determined by the cooking method (for example, the toasty flavors of a stir fry), the sauce (from curries to sweet-and-sour), the use of seasonings (such as ginger and coriander leaves to mask fishy tastes), or the blending of ingredients to form new flavors (as in sukiyaki or satay). Indeed, it may result from a combination of any of these elements.

With these challenges in mind, this book presents a unique and straightforward way of matching wine with Asian foods. We have organized the varied flavors that are typical of Eastern cuisines into five categories that form the basis for our method. We have also examined the fundamental characteristics of a large number of wines and categorized these by style.

We did this to provide an easy cross-reference to the wine types suitable for each of the five flavors. Therefore, pairing a given wine style with one of our categories of food flavors will enable you to match wines with a spectrum of Asian dishes quickly, easily, and successfully.

The fifty recipes we have compiled offer the authentic tastes and pleasures of dishes from China, Japan, Southeast Asia, and India. They are classic Asian dishes and are, therefore, commonly found in restaurants. These recipes have also been selected with the intention that they may be easily and successfully prepared at home, whether you live in Asia or not. Using the recipes and tasting the food with the recommended wines will help you understand the matching mechanism and give you the confidence to serve wine with any Asian dish.

You will notice that the recipes are arranged according to the flavor profile of the dishes. We have softened the arbitrary boundaries of country and have, instead, grouped the dishes according to their flavor profile because this is the determining factor when selecting a wine for Asian cuisines.

Each recipe is accompanied by wine pairing suggestions that include choices from European and New World vineyards. Moreover, a general suggestion of the appropriate wine style is given (such as Woody Whites or Light and Fruity Reds). This means that if our choice of the best wine for the dish is not available, you can pick from a list of alternatives. This gives you a good chance of finding a suitable wine at your neighborhood wine shop or in your favorite restaurant.

We have included the names of particular producers in our wine suggestions. These are the producers whose products we have tried over a period of many years and who have consistently maintained a high level of quality. They

A wide variety of spices and herbs go into the making of complex-tasting Indonesian gravies and pastes.

are but a tiny portion of the world's excellent wine producers. We urge you to try other famous and not-so-famous names in order to find your own favorites.

We have also included recipes for a set of Asian finger foods that represent the cuisines of a spectrum of different countries, selected according to our categories of flavor. Use them when you entertain or as a basis for tastings to discover exciting new pairings.

There is a real joy in combining wine with Asian food, as the process gives you the chance to explore new regions, grape varieties, and styles. Join us now in this delicious gastronomic journey of discovery.

LAYERS OF BOLD FLAVORS

Asian cuisines are often multitextured and combine overlapping layers of bold flavors. Wine and food writers are all too likely to dismiss the challenge of matching wine with such foods with a shrug and the facile suggestion: "Drink beer!" If pressed, they often mutter "Gewürztraminer," which is like saying that Cabernet Sauvignon is great with American food – never mind that it might not be the best match for New England clam chowder, Southern fried chicken, California brook trout, Crab Jambalaya, boiled Gefilte fish, or Bean and Jalapeno Chimichangos.

Admittedly, when finding a wine partner for Asian food, you cannot always take the straight, well-traveled route of matching the wine to the primary ingredient: full-bodied red with meat and dry white with shellfish. Instead, you need to pick a wine to harmonize with the predominant *flavor* of a dish – be it derived from a blend of spices, a cooking method, or a sauce.

In the following paragraphs, we examine the five basic flavors – salty, sour, sweet, bitter, umami – and their impact upon wine. We also examine the role that texture and cooking techniques plays in determining flavor and matching in general.

Salty

The saltiness of soy and oyster sauces will be accentuated by the tannin and alcohol of red wines. Hence, that restaurant mainstay, Cabernet Sauvignon, may not be an ideal choice to accompany an Asian meal. Rather, it is best to choose a red wine with softer tannins, such as one made from Merlot, Pinot Noir, or Nero d'Avola. An alternative might be a lighter style Nebbiolo from the northern Italian zone of Valtellina.

These wines offer rich, broadly fruity flavors and a softness on the palate that will not clash with a salty flavored sauce. Well-structured rosés, too (such as Bardolino Chiaretto and Tavel), with their attractive fragrances and much lower tannin levels, make excellent partners because they subdue the salty flavors found in soy sauce, oyster sauce, shrimp paste, and bean paste.

Just as the flavor of fish is often enhanced by a squeeze of lemon juice, some salty foods seem brighter and more appealing when partnered with tangy wines (such as a dry Riesling from the Mosel or New Zealand Sauvignon Blanc) or dry sparkling wines (those labeled Brut or Extra Brut).

Champagne, for example, with its lively acidity acts as a good foil for saltiness – just think of the classic pairing of Champagne and oysters. Be aware that the saltiness in food will make lightly sweet wines (examples might be Moscato d'Asti or a medium-sweet Chenin Blanc from South Africa) appear to taste even sweeter.

Top left and center: There are many types of limes in Southeast Asia. They contribute to the tangy nuances of Thai, Laotian, and Vietnamese salads.

Top right: Tubs of Chinese preserved vegetables give a salty, earthy flavor.

Bitter

Bitter constituents in Asian food may come from roasted nuts, the char of a hot wok, or the bitterness of some green vegetables such as bitter gourd and arugula. Bitterness in food seems to increase the bitterness in the wine. For that reason, it is best to pay attention to "herbaceous" characteristics in a wine: A little bitterness goes a long, long way. That is why just any Sauvignon Blanc is not the best choice for Asian cuisines. If you really crave Sauvignon Blanc, it is best to chose one with a softer, more tropical fruit character, such as those found in Chile and Australia, or better still, a Vouvray, or a lightly sweet Riesling from the Rheingau, Mittelrhein, or Pfalz, or a lighter Italian Trebbiano or Pinot Grigio.

Sour

Sourness is often considered an attractive flavor in Asian cultures. It may be derived from such ingredients as tamarind, lime juice, and unripe mangoes. Wines with zesty acidity (such as Verdicchio or sparkling Durello, French Mâcon Villages, Alsace Edelzwicker, Muscadet, Austrian Schilcher, and Trocken German Riesling or Scheurebe) will make a sour-flavored food seem richer and rounder.

Sweet

Sweetness – coming from fresh and dried fruits or sugared and coconut milk-based sauces – is an element that assumes a much more prominent role in Asian cuisines than in Western cooking. Sweet foods tend to make a dry wine seem, at best, drier or, at worst, thin and sour. A medium-sweet wine (such as a Riesling from the Rheinhessen or a demi-sec Vouvray), or, depending on the dish, even a fully sweet wine (like Sélection de Grains Nobles

Facing, top left: The bittergourd, as its name states, is bitter – much more so than Brussel sprouts.

Facing, bottom right: Eggplants come in different shapes and sizes, but they are all bitter.

Top left: Indian curry leaves are used only in certain curries to provide a specific tanginess and bitter edge. As a garnish, the leaves are fried in hot oil for their aroma.

Top right: Chinese kailan stems have some bitterness.

Facing, top left:
Chinese sausages, or
"waxed sausages", are
preserved till they are
hard. They have a
smoky, sweet, and salty
taste.

Facing, bottom left:
Mushrooms, used dried
and fresh in a Chinese
kitchen, are a source of
umami.

Gewürztraminer from Alsace), would be a better choice. The silky textures and concentrated fragrances of these wines fit comfortably alongside the richness of a sweet dish. A dry, high acid wine would tend to taste harsh on the palate when paired with sweetish foods or sauces.

The Sweet and Sour Combination

With a sweet and sour flavor combination it is essentially the sweet element that takes the lead when it comes to choosing a wine. It is wisest to choose lightly sweet and sweet wines with good body and firm acidity, such as Mosel Riesling Auslese and other off-dry Rieslings, Gewürztraminers, and Chenin Blancs.

Umami

Umami, derived from the Japanese word for "delicious," is a rich, meaty, and savory flavor associated with glutamate. Although it is a newly defined flavor in the West (hence, it has come to be referred to as the fifth taste), it has been known to Japanese chefs for more than a century.

Umami is sometimes added to Asian dishes in the form of monosodium glutamate, which was originally derived from seaweed. It is also found naturally in many Asian and Western food ingredients such as cured meat, caviar, fermented soy products, ripe tomatoes, mushrooms, and asparagus. The umami characteristics are concentrated when foods are fermented, dried, or cured. It is a also a major flavor in oyster sauce and fish sauce.

Umami will make the alcohol in a wine seem stronger and can bring out metallic tastes. When umami is the defining characteristic of a dish, it is best to serve a sweetish wine that is low in alcohol. Moscato d'Asti (with its alcohol level of around 5 percent) and many nondry German wines fall into this type.

A trio of Asian spices: Pepper, chilis, and ginger. Green peppercorns are used in such Thai dishes as Jungle Curry, while chilis are ubiquitous, to provide heat. Young ginger has a fresher flavor than old ginger.

However, the delicate salinity and mineral elements often found in white wines made from indigenous European varieties (such as Nuragus, Vermentino, Fiano, and Falanghina from Italy, and Portuguese Alvarinho and Spanish Albariño) can also merge well and even enhance the umami characteristics. This makes perfect sense when we remember that a dash of salt or a salty condiment, like soy sauce, can calm the umami flavor.

Also, aged Pinot Noirs have a surprising knack of bringing out the best in umami-rich ingredients, such as mussels, cured fish, lobster, and mushrooms.

Chili Heat

The hot sensation arising from chili spices is part of the appeal of many Asian foods. A lightly sweet wine can sooth the palate, calming the chili burn, but a highly alcoholic wine, sweet or otherwise, may accentuate the fieriness as alcohol dissolves the chili and spreads it around the mouth.

It is often best to choose lightly sweet wines with lowish alcohol, such as Brachetto d'Acqui, Moscato d'Asti, and Orvieto Abboccato from Italy, Austrian Grüner Veltliner Spätlese, Riesling Spätlese from the Mosel region of Germany, and a White Zinfandel from California.

The sweetness in the wine tends to envelop the chili and neutralize any aggressive heat while enhancing the true flavor of the dish. Sweeter sparkling wines and demi-sec Champagnes also appeal to some chili lovers. The effervescence of such sparkling wines creates a lively tingle on the palate that echoes that of the sensation created by the chili. This doubles the sensual pleasure for chili fans.

Some chili dishes also work well with chilled (we mean really, really cold) fruity reds, such as Beaujolais and Dolcetto.

Do not try to match chili-rich dishes with high-tannin wines, like young Bordeaux and Cabernet Sauvignon. The tannins tend to collide with the chili heat, producing an unpleasant flavor.

If you really crave a great big red, go for wines with softer tannins and luscious fruitiness, such as wines made from Zwiegelt, Merlot, or Pinot Noirs or such Italian reds as Montepulciano d'Abruzzo, Rosso Picenos, and Rosso Coneros. Note that the tangy acidity of dry wines will accentuate the chili sensation.

Top: In rural communities throughout Asia, kitchen gardens are informal and wild, a place where herbs and spices can share beds with flowering plants.

THE TEXTURE OF WINE

Wines can be smooth and velvety (such as sweet wines and mature red wines), chewy and tannic (certain young red wines), or lively and bubbly (sparkling wines). They also have body, that is, "weight" in the mouth. This weight is determined in part by the amount of alcohol in the wine.

You can imagine full-bodied wines as having a texture and weight in the mouth similar to that of milky coffee. Medium-bodied wine is similar to a fruit tea, and light-bodied wine is similar to lime juice. In wine, the alcohol element is balanced by other components, such as sweetness, acidity, or tartness, flavor, and other constituents, such as tannin.

Food can be crunchy (vegetables), crisp (tempura, with its fried batter), silky (steamed fish), savory (coming from salty flavors derived from fish sauce, fermented soy beans, or oyster sauce), or creamy (from the use of coconut milk). Often it is a good idea to look for similar textures in the wine and the food served.

Pacific Rim Dry Ries
BONNY DOON VINEYARD

COOKING TECHNIQUES

Cooking techniques add an additional layer of flavor as well. Stir frying gives a smoky, nutty nuance, which calls for a wine with good body or a similarly toasty flavor, such as Meursault or an oak-aged Chardonnay, a Fino or Amontillado Sherry or, perhaps, a Bual Madeira.

Deep frying or pan frying adds an oily sensation that requires the crisp, palate-cleansing properties provided by whites fermented in stainless steel, such as an unoaked Chardonnay, Muscadet de Sèvre et Maine, or a Soave. A lightly sweet sparkling Prosecco, a demi-sec Champagne, or New World sparkler, whose effervescence creates the same kind of clean, fresh sensation, may also make a good partner for deep-fried foods.

Stewed and braised dishes call for wines that will echo their rich flavors and dense textures, such as a Nero d'Avola or a lightly oaked Pinot Noir from California.

The softer, slightly smoky flavors of grilled vegetables, fish, and chicken call for zesty, fruity wines such as a good Australian Semillion-Sauvignon blend. When red meat is grilled, it is best to choose one of the many fruity, soft-tannin reds that have recently become popular. You will never go wrong with a good Merlot.

The often delicate flavors of steamed foods will be enhanced by lighter wine styles, which mirror the foods' purity and freshness. An ideal match can be made with whites from the Italian region of Friuli (from such varieties as Sauvignon Blanc, Ribolla Gialla, and Pinot Grigio), from New Zealand and from the northwestern United States (Oregon, Washington, and northern California).

Top left: This attractive wine gift bag of Chinese design testifies to the growing popularity of wine drinking in Asia.

Top: Not to be mistaken for two small bottles of wine, these are bottles of high-grade Japanese shoyu, or soya sauce.

Left: The clean palate of sushi contrasts sharply with the deep, rich taste of food seasoned with oyster sauce. Such differences that can appear in dishes served at the same time in an Asian meal poses a challenge to choosing one wine to match all dishes.

NEW APPROACHES TO ENJOYING
WINE WITH ASIAN FOOD

Communal dining, in which many dishes are served at the same time and shared by everyone at the table, is the traditional way of serving Asian meals. As every diner has a slightly different mixture of flavors and textures on his or her plate, the wine chosen for such a meal has to be versatile. If you wish to serve only one wine at a communal meal, our experience has shown us that the most "Asian food-friendly" wine category is juicy whites, medium rosés, and light reds (Category 2).

However, we suggest that, when possible, you have both a red (or rosé) and a white wine on the table. We also urge you to have a crisp sweet wine as well. When mingled with hot-chili flavors, a sweet wine creates a wonderfully rich, rounded sensation on the palate. Be adventurous in matching communal food and wines, sipping the appropriate wine as you taste the different dishes on the table. This approach presents wonderful opportunities for enjoying – and discovering – food and wine matches.

For communal dining, avoid big, highly tannic reds and oaky whites at all costs. These wines make wonderful partners for specific dishes, but their taste profiles do not accommodate many fish or seafood dishes or sweet and sour sauces.

When having Asian food at a restaurant or at home, you can arrange to have the dishes served in courses, Western style. This will give you control as to which wine you serve with each dish, exactly as you would for a traditional Western meal.

THE FLAVOR SYSTEM

Five Food Flavors

As we analyzed the flavors in Asian dishes, we came to realize that they could easily be split into five basic categories: Fresh & Herbal, Savory & Rich, Mildly Spicy & Light Smoky, Spicy & Smoky, and Fiery & Sweet. The sections below list ingredients, cooking methods, and sauces that typify a specific flavor range. Every recipe has wine suggestions, which include selections from Europe and the New World.

Seven Categories of Wine Styles

We tasted wines from around the world, analyzing their flavor, texture, and body. After classifying the wines, we began to taste them with dishes from the five flavor categories to understand more fully how the wines reacted with food. From this research emerged our wine selector classification, which consists of seven categories: 1. Crisp wines and dry aromatic wines, 2. Juicy whites, medium rosés, and light reds, 3. Woody whites and soft-tannin reds, 4. Light to medium-sweet wines, 5. Richly sweet wines, 6. Red wines with chewy tannin, and 7. Nutty and rich, fortified wines. These classifications provide you with a technique for matching food flavors with wine styles.

We have tried to synthesize our knowledge to make it easy for you to make matching decisions. Will some of you disagree with some of our wine suggestions? Of course. Our method for matching wine and food is intended as a guide – a framework that gives you a sound foundation from which to try new pairings.

Tamarind, or asam, is the fruit of the *Tamarindus indica* tree. The raw pod with its pale green flesh (top left) is dried, and the resulting brown pulp (top right) is used as an ingredient to give food a tart taste. This pulp, with seeds and fibers removed, is sold in packets. Tamarind is not to be confused with asam gelugor which is of the *Garcinia atroviridis* variety. Asam gelugor, sliced into thin rings and dried (top right), produces a sour flavor similar to tamarind.

THE FIVE FLAVORS

Facing, top left: The leaves and rind of the kaffir lime, also known as leperous lime, grant Southeast Asian dishes an incomparable flavor.

Facing, top right: Several types of basil are used in Southeast Asia, with the leaves added at the end of the cooking process to obtain a balanced and fresh fragrance.

Facing, bottom right: Choy sum, or Chinese mustard greens, are served stir-fried, steamed and in soups.

Facing, bottom left: Tart and crunchy unripe mangoes are used in Thai salads.

Top right: Candlenuts or buah keras, when used to thicken curries, add a subtle flavor.

Fresh & Herbal Flavors

These are the bright, crisp flavors of fresh herbs, leaves, and vegetables and the fruity tartness of lemons, limes, unripe mangoes, and tamarind. They include the tangy tastes found in vinegar and salty fish sauce that are used to balance and enliven dishes.

Herbs and seasonings: basil, leaf cilantro, lemongrass, limes, and kaffir lime leaves.

Cooking methods: boiling (white meats), steaming, poaching (fresh and saltwater fish), stir frying (including vegetables in light batter), and crisp batter frying. Raw food also falls within this category.

Sauces: condiments and dipping sauces with tart or salty characteristics, such as fish sauce, lemon juice, and lime juice.

Wines to serve with fresh and herbal flavors: crisp wines and dry, aromatic wines (white, red, and rosé, both still and sparkling) from Category 1.

Dry, tart wines clean the palate and brighten the flavor of fishy, salty, oily, and stir-fried foods in the same way that a few drops of lemon juice lift and define the flavors in a salad. Their tangy sensations also echo those of fresh, zesty herbs. Their straightforward fragrances and flavors do not overpower the delicate nature of steamed or poached foods. When these wines are served with pickle relishes (such as those that accompany raw fish and plain rice) or pomelo, their acidity is tamed, and they may seem lightly sweet.

Savory & Rich Flavors

This is the realm of dark rich spices and sauces, onion and meat stocks,

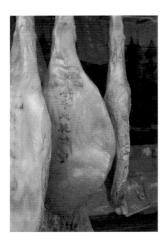

dishes based on red meats, and meaty mushrooms.

Herbs and seasonings: star anise, nutmeg, roasted coriander seeds, cinnamon, cardamom, mustard seeds, fenugreek, and cloves.

Cooking methods: roasting (red meats), barbecuing, stewing (red meats), grilling (red meats), heavy smoking, charring, or blackening (meats).

Sauces: rich barbecue sauce, mustard, sweet soy sauce, oyster sauce, mushroom sauce, and nut-based sauces.

Wines to serve with savory and rich flavors: chewy, high-tannin red wines from Category 6.

Youthful tannic reds love fatty foods. The tannins bind with the fat in the food, making the wine seem smoother and rounder, and the food more succulent.

Mildly Spicy & Light Smoky Flavors

These are the flavors of mellow spices and the soft tastes and textures of yogurt and coconut milk.

Herbs and seasonings: allspice, candlenut, coconut, coriander seeds, fennel, ginger, saffron, mint, raw nuts (whole or ground), sesame oil.

Cooking methods: baking, deep frying (seafood and vegetables), roasting (vegetables), grilling (vegetables, fish, and chicken), smoking (fish), braising and stewing (tofu), and making mild curries such as sayor lodeh.

Sauces: yogurt-based sauces, coconut milk-based sauces, mild curries.

Wines to serve with mildly spicy and light smoky flavors: juicy white wines, medium rosé wines and light red wines from Category 2, and aromatic wines from Category 1.

The round, palate-pleasing fruit balanced by the crisp acidity that characterizes juicy whites, medium-bodied rosés, and light reds provides a foil for

Top left: Chinese air-dried ham is rock solid. The best qualilty is said to be from Yunnan Province.

Top center: The bright orange tumeric rhizome is used fresh in Southeast Asian cooking, but it is also available dried and ground.

Far left: Chefs at a breakfast buffet preparing paper-thin dosai, one of many types of Indian breads.

Left: Roast duck and other roasted meats such as char siew are common fare in Chinese restuarants.

the softer, slightly smoky flavors of roasted, grilled, and baked dishes. The lively fruity and floral fragrances of lightly sweet aromatic wines lift the flavors of mildly spicy food while refreshing the palate. If ginger is the key seasoning, sweetish aromatic wines are the best foil for the spice's tingling flavor.

Spicy and Smoky Flavors

These flavors reflect the warm, rich qualities of spices like cumin, nutmeg, and the delicate-yet-nutty flavors shared by batter-fried dishes and foods cooked in a tandoori oven or roasted, broiled, or grilled on charcoal or wood.

Herbs and seasonings: mild chilis, cumin, nutmeg, mace, tamarind, turmeric, saffron, and sesame seeds (paste and oil).

Cooking methods: boiling (red meats), grilling (pork, white meats, seafood, and meaty fish), braising (pork, red meats, and meaty fish), roasting (pork, red meats, lobster, and meaty fish), stewing (pork, red meats, and meaty fish), smoking (meats), deep frying (red meats), stir frying (noodles and seafood), marsala curries, tandoori, and batter frying (vegetables, seafood, and meats).

Sauces: peanut sauce and rich nut-based sauces in general, curry paste, sesame paste, garlic chili sauce, oyster sauce, and tamarind paste.

Wines to serve with spicy and smoky flavors: woody white wines and fruity soft-tannin red wines from Category 3 and the nutty and rich fortified wines of Category 7.

Category 3 wines: white wines aged in wood develop spicy, vanilla notes that echo the nutmeg and cinnamon spices in this category. The versatility of soft-tannin reds allows them to softly underscore the qualities of pork, meaty fish, and seafood.

Category 7 wines: the flavors associated with stir frying and those derived from sesame oil, sesame seeds, and roasted nuts are echoed by the rich tones of Fino sherry and other dry fortified wines.

Fiery & Sweet Flavors

These are the flavors of food seasoned with chilies, whose heat is often tempered by a touch of sweetness from sugar, honey, ripe fruits, or coconut milk. This category also includes foods with some sweetness.

Herbs and seasonings: hot chili, cloves, sugar, and palm sugar.

Cooking methods: any method whereby the spicy hotness or rich sweetness of a dish is accentuated.

Sauces: chili paste, hot curry paste, Hoisin sauce, kechap manis, mirin, sweet and sour sauce, sweet soy sauce, teriyaki sauce, pungent fish sauce, chutney, and sauces made from fresh or dried fruits.

Wines to serve with spicy or sweet flavors: light- to medium-sweet wines (medium-dry, off-dry), white, red, and rosé, still and sparkling, from Category 4. Richly sweet wines, both white and red, from Category 5. Also well-chilled fruity reds from Category 2.

Category 4: this category is often neglected when matching wine with Western foods. However, within the context of Asian dishes, lightly sweet wines are given a chance to shine. They underscore the sweet notes found in many Asian dishes (a result of coconut milk, sugar, or dried fruit), and their sweetness enfolds mild spices and hot sensations, creating interesting textural matches or contrasts with the food. Sweet wines soothe the palate after the burst of chili spice and heat and prepares the mouth for the next bite.

Some chili lovers like to drink very, very cold sparkling wines. They find

Top, far left: A tiny bird's eye chili on the plant. Generally, the smaller the chili, the higher the heat.

Top center: Asian chefs closely guard their curry powder recipes. The secret is in the proportion of chili and one or more other ground ingredients such as turmeric, coriander, cumin, and nutmeg.

Top: A display of pepper among a cornucopia of dried spices.

the combination of the wine's effervesce and the chili's tingle exciting. As it is the sensation rather than the nuance of fruit and flavor that makes this partnership work, it is best to choose inexpensive sparklers.

Category 5: when the predominant flavor of a dish is sweet, you should pick a wine that is at least as sweet as the dish itself. Do not be afraid to try a richly sweet wine, one you would usually think of pairing with dessert. This style also envelops the chili in sour and salty dishes.

Some chili dishes also work with very well chilled fruity reds, such as Beaujolais or Bardolino from Category 2.

THE SEVEN WINE STYLES

To provide readers with the best possible chance of finding a wine at their local shop or restaurant to match their Asian meal, we have included a list of well-known wine zones and grape varieties.

You will notice that the wines are not organized in the traditional way: the whites together followed by all the reds. Instead the seven wine styles are arranged according to their weight (the impression of substance that the wine expresses in the mouth), their level of sweetness, and their balancing acidity.

As Italy and France are major wine producers, these countries are listed first under the Europe category. If Old World means Europe, New World has come to mean everywhere else, from Australia to Argentina, from the United States to Uruguay. As New World wines are often varietals, we list the appropriate grape varieties, as well as the specialty wines of countries, when applicable.

Because of the virtual absence of appellation rules (rules that give some

idea of the style of wine that you can expect) in New World countries, we suggest that you read the label on the back of the wine bottle or take the advice of a trusted wine merchant when it comes to determining the style of a wine with which you are unfamiliar.

In our wine categories we refer to oaked and unoaked wines. "Oaked" wines are those that have been aged (or even fermented) in wood barrels. The presence or absence of wood makes a big difference in the flavor and weight of a wine. Oaked wines tend to have a layer of spicy flavor (nutmeg, vanilla) and are fuller bodied. "Unoaked" wines tend to offer fruity flavors and a crisp, fresh style.

CATEGORY 1
Crisp wines and dry, aromatic wines.
This wine style is often a good match for dishes with a fresh and herbal flavor.

Sparkling
Europe
Blanquette de Limoux sec

Brut Blanc de Blancs Champagne

Brut Cava (Spain)

Brut Champagne

Brut Prosecco (Italy)

Brut Rosé Champagne

Brut Saumur

Cremant de Die

Franciacorta (Italy)

New World
Brut sparklers in general

. . . .

White
Europe
Albana di Romagna

Bianco di Custoza

Chablis

Clairette de Die

Clairette du Languedoc

Entre-Deux-Mers

Frascati

Friulian dry varietal
wines in general (Italy)

Gros Plant du Pays Nantias

Jasnieres

Mâcon Villages

Muscadet

Petit Chablis

Picpoul de Pinet

Pouilly-Fumé

Sancerre

Santorini sec/dry (Greece)

Sauvignon de Touraine

Savennières

CATEGORY 1

White: *Europe*

Scheurebe Trocken (Germany)
Schilcher (Austria)
Verdicchio
Vin de Savoie
Vinho Verde (Portugal)
Unoaked Soave

New World

Unoaked dry wines such
as Chardonnay and other
aromatic varieties

. . . .

Rosé

Europe

Clairet de Bordeaux
Patrimonio (France)
Rosé d' Anjou
Rosé de Loire
Sancerre Rosé

New World

Unoaked varietals based on
   Grenache
   Pinot Noir
   Cabernet Franc
Unoaked Vin Gris

Still, Dry Aromatic Wines

Dry wines made from
   Gewürztraminer
   Muscat
   Riesling
   Sauvignon Blanc

WORDS DENOTING SWEETNESS

The words that denote levels of sweetness in sparkling wines vary from country to country and are often confusing (if not misleading). The most commonly used terms are:

Brut Zero (Brut nature, Dosage Zero, Brut Sauvage) – the driest style of sparkling wine

Extra Brut – very dry

Brut – dry

Extra-sec – off-dry to lightly sweet

Demi-sec – sweet

Doux – very sweet

German and Austrian wine words from dry to sweet:

Troken – dry

Halbtrocken – lightly sweet

Kabinett – dry to very lightly sweet

Spätlese – medium-sweet

Auslese – sweet

Beerenauslese – very sweet

Trokenbeerenauslese – extremely sweet

Eiswein – extremely sweet and rich, with zippy acidity

Other terms found on labels:

Botritis cinerea – Noble Rot

Pourriture Noble – Noble Rot

Sélection Grains Nobles – Noble Rot

Moelleux – medium sweet

Puttonyos – Hungarian measure of sweetness

CATEGORY 2   Juicy white wines, medium rosé wines, and light red wines, sparkling and still. This wine style often makes a good match for dishes with a mildly spicy and light smoky flavor profile.

Sparkling
Europe

Consider the following Crémant-style sparkling wines, which have a frothier, more mouth-filling sensation rendering them softer and seemingly more fruity.

  Blanquette méthode ancestrale
  Bugey
    Crémant d'Alsace
    Crémant de Bourgogne
    Crémant de Loire
    Crémant de Limoux
    Crémant du Jura
      (blanc and rosé)
    Franciacorta Saten (Italy)
    Vouvray Mousseux

New World

Rosé sparkling wines in general, also Sparkling Shiraz and Sparkling Cabernet (Australia)

. . . .

White
Europe

Albariño (Spain)
Alsace Pinot Blanc
Alsace Pinot Gris
Anjou Blanc
Cassis
Chablis Grand Cru

Chasselas (Switzerland)
Corton-Charlemagne
Falanghina
Fiano d'Avellino
Greco di Tufo
Grüner Veltliner (Austria)

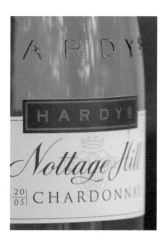

CATEGORY 2

White: *Europe*

Hermitage Blanc

Lugana (Italy)

Müller-Thurgau (Germany)

Nuragus (Italy)

Pinot Grigio

Pessac-Léognan

Quincy

Scheurebe

Trebbiano

Vermentino

Viura (Spain)

White Burgundies

White Graves

White Rioja (Spain)

New World

Very lightly oaked wines based
on the varietals

  Chardonnay

  Chenin Blanc

  Colombard

  Pinot Blanc

  Semillon (oaked)

  Torrontes Muscat (Argentina)

Rosés

Europe

Arbois Poulsard Clairet

Bandol Rosé

Bardolino Chiaretto

Bergerac Rosé

Ciró Rosato (Italy)

Floc de Gascogne Rosé (France)

Lirac

Montepulciano d'Abruzzo
  Cerasuolo

Reuilly Rosé

Rosada Navarra (Spain)

Rosé de Provence

Rosé des Riceys

Tavel

CATEGORY 2 **Rosés**

New World

Unoaked or lightly oaked
wines based on the varietals

   Barbera

   Cabernet Franc

   Carignan

   Gamay

   Grenache

Merlot

Pinot Noir

*New Zealand, northern California,
and the cooler areas of Australia offer
good pink wines from these varieties.*

· ·

Reds

Europe

Alsace Pinot Noir

Bardolino

Beaujolais

Bellet Rouge

Blaufränkisch (Austria)

Bonarda

Bourgueil Rouge (France)

Cabernet d'Anjou

Carema

Chinon

Corbières Rouge

Côte du Rhône

Dolcetto

Dry Lambrusco

Mercurey

Red Burgundies such as

   Bourgogne Rouge

   Bourgogne Passe Tout Grains

Sancerre Rouge

Santenay Rouge

Saumur-Champigny

Teroldego

Touraine Rouge

Valtellina (Italy)

Young Ciró

Young St. Emillion

CATEGORY 2   **Reds**

New World

Wines based on the varietals	Merlot
Barbera	Pinot Noir
Cabernet Franc	
Carignan	*California, Oregon, and Washington excel in wines made from these varieties, as do the cool climate areas of Australia. Chile excels in Merlots.*
Gamay	
Grenache	

CATEGORY 3   Woody white wines and fruity soft-tannin red wines.

This wine style often makes a good match for dishes with mildly spicy and light smoky or spicy and smoky flavors.

Whites

Europe

Chateau Grillet

Condrieu

Soave Superiore (Italy)

Trebbiano d'Abruzzo

Verdicchio Superiore

Vin de Pays Chardonnay (France)

White Burgundies such as

  Meursault

  Montrachet

  Puligny-Montrachet

New World

Oaked varietals based on

  Chardonnay

  Pinot Blanc

  Semillon-Sauvignon blends

  Viognier

Australia California, Chile, Oregon, and Washington excel in wines made from these varieties. Australia's Semillion-Sauvignon blends are particularly good.

. . . .

Reds

Europe

Barbera

Chianti

Rosso Conero

Rosso di Montalcino

Rosso di Montepulciano

Rosso Piceno

Valpolicella Ripasso

Valtellina Superiore

Young Sangiovese

CATEGORY 3

Reds: *Europe*

Bairrada (Portugal)

Beaujolais Crus

Duero (Spain)

Hautes Côtes de Beaune

Hautes Côtes de Nuits

Moderately aged
  St. Émilion

Montepulciano

Nero d'Avola (Italy)

Ribera Del Duero (Spain)

Young Rioja(Spain)

Young Tempranillo (Spain)

New World

Grenache-Shiraz blends

Petit Sirah

Shiraz-Cabernet blends

Varietals of Merlot

Varietals of Pinot Noir

*Look to Australia for
outstanding Shiraz blends.*

CATEGORY 4   Light to medium-sweet wines (medium dry, off-dry).
This wine style is often a good match for dishes with fiery and sweet flavors.

Sparkling

Europe

Asti (Spumante)

Brachetto

Cartizze

Demi-sec Champage (France)

Demi Secco Cava (Spain)

Sweet Lambrusco (Italy)

New World

Sparkling wines with "demi-sec"
    or "semi-sweet" on the label

Sparkling white Zinfandel

. . . .

White

Europe

Cadillac (France)

Côteaux du Layon

Demi-Sec Vouvray

Loupiac

Moscatel (Spain)

Moscato d'Asti (Italy)

Spätlese and Auslese (Germany)

New World

Medium-sweet Chenin Blanc

Medium-sweet Gewürztraminer

Medium-sweet Riesling

*In South Africa Chenin Blanc
sometimes goes under the name
"Steen."*

CATEGORY 4

Rosé

Europe

Wines with the word
"saignee" on the label
Portuguese rosé
German Weissherbst
  (sweet version)

New World

Pink or blush wines, such as
  White Merlot
  White Shiraz
  White Zinfandel
  Zinfandel Rosé
  Wines with the term "free run"

. . . .

Red

New World

Tarrango (Australia)

CATEGORY 5   Richly sweet wines.

This wine style often makes a good match for dishes with a fiery and sweet flavor profile.

White
Europe
Barsac

Beerenauslese

Eiswein (Germany and Austria)

Monbazilliac

Moscatel de Setubal (Portugal)

Moscatel de Valencia (Spain)

Muscat, red, rosé, white
(Ukraine and Moldovia)

Muscat de Beaumes-de-Venise

Passito di Pantelleria

Quarts-de-Chaume

Recioto di Soave

St. Croix du Monts

Sauternes

Sélection de Grains Nobles
Gewürztraminer (France)

Sweet Passito wines (Italy)

Tokaji (Hungary)

Trockenberenauslese

Vendange Tardive Alsace Riesling

New World
Californian Black Muscats

Late-harvest varietals such as
Canadian Ice Wine
Late-harvest Gewürztraminers
Late-harvest Semillons
Orange Muscat

Wines with the names "cordon cut,"
"botrytis," and "vin de glacière"
on the label.

· · · · · · · · · · · · · · · · · · · ·

Red
Europe
Mavrodaphne (Greek)

Recioto della Valpolicella (Italy)

Sweet red wines from the New World are rare.

CATEGORY 6   Red wines with chewy tannin.

This category is often a good match for dishes with savory and rich flavors.

Red

Europe

Barbaresco

Barbera in barrique

Barolo

Bordeaux Supérieur (France)

Brunello di Montalcino (Italy)

Cabernet Sauvignons from
   Estremadura or Ribatejano
   regions (Portugal)

Cahors

Carmignano

Châteauneuf du Pape

Chianti Classico

Cornas

Côte Rôtie

Gigondas

Hermitage

Madiran

Mavrud (Bulgaria)

Negroamaro

Rioja
   Gran Riserva and Riserva

Riversaltes

Sagrantino

St. Joseph

"Super Tuscans"

Taurasi

Vino Nobile di Montepulciano

Zwiegelt (Austria)

New World

Barbera

Cabernet Sauvignon

Carmenère

Malbec

Mouvèdre

Pinotage

Shiraz

Tannat

Zinfandel

Zinfandel is a speciality of California, Shiraz of Australia, and Pinotage of South Africa.

CATEGORY 7

Nutty and rich fortified wines

Dry fortified wines can enhance the nutty flavor of some deep-fried dishes. For example, there are those who enjoy matching tempura with Fino Sherry. The style may also be matched with stir fries, peanut sauces, and hot-and-sour Malaysian curries.

The very adventurous among you may wish to try pairing richly fortified wines that are sweet, such as Cream Sherry, Vintage Malmsey, and even port. It is safe to say that with these combinations you are truly venturing into the realm of personal taste. Go there by all means.

Dry Styles

Europe

Fino Sherry

Manzanilla Sherry (Spain)

Macvin du Jura

Sercial Madeira

Verdelho Madiera

Vin Jaune

Vin Santo (Italy)

New World

Dry "Sherries"

Fortified Muscats

. . . .

Sweet Styles

Europe

Amontillado Sherry

Banyuls (France)

Colheita Port

Commandaria (Cyprus)

Malmsey Maderia

Málaga (Spain)

Oloroso Sherry

Palo Cortado Sherry

Pedro Ximinez Sherry (Spain)

CATEGORY 7   **Sweet Styles:** *Europe*

Pineau des Charentes (France)

Rasteau

Ruby Port (Portugal)

Sweet Marsala (Italy)

Tawny Port

Vintage Character Port

New World

Cream Sherry

Fortified Muscats (Australia)

   Brown Muscat

   Frontignan

   Liqueur Muscat

   Liqueur Tokay

Port

Sweet Sherry

Muscat de Beaumes de Venice is a lightly fortified wine and therefore belongs in Category 5.

Premium
BOTTLE FERMENTED
ESTABLISHED 1847
JACOB'S CREEK
Sparkling Rosé
Jacob's Creek, site of Johann Gramp's
in the Barossa Valley

THE RELATIVITY OF TASTE

When you combine wine with food, you are seeking a balance between these two elements. This can be achieved either by their having similar characteristics or opposite ones. You should bear in mind, however, that the sensation you experience will be conditioned by what you have tasted immediately beforehand.

One of the best ways to understand this interaction is to do a little experiment. Take a slice of ripe, red apple, a slice of lemon, and a small piece of neutral-flavored cheese (asiago, edam, or processed cheddar). Then pour yourself a glass of white wine and a glass of red wine. First, taste the white wine. Close your eyes and try to really think about its flavor. Then nibble the slice of apple and taste the wine again. The wine will taste sour and have a harsh texture. Next, suck on the wedge of lemon and then taste the wine immediately afterward. The wine will usually seem sweeter and take on a smoother texture. Now take a sip of red wine. When you have a clear idea of the wine's flavor, eat a small piece of cheese. You should find a dramatic difference: the wine will seem fuller, rounder, and much less acidic.

Taste Tests with Asian ingredients

To understand the interaction of specifically Asian flavors, we have selected ingredients that represent each of our flavor profiles. You can conduct experiments with these ingredients similar to the ones described above. First, try the specified ingredient with the wine category we have suggested. Then try it with the wines from other categories.

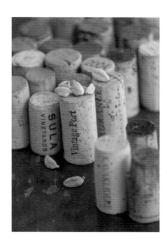 

Facing, top left: Oyster sauce or *ho yau* in **Cantonese is thick and salty. Caramel contributes to its rich brown color.**

Facing, top right: Chili pastes form the basis of many dishes in Southeast Asian and Indian cuisine.

Facing, bottom right: Pappad or papadam are spicy Indian crackers made from gram flour, chilis and spices. They are deep fried just before serving.

Facing, bottom left: Kalamansi lime has a piquant flavor. It tempers chili heat and is therefore commonly served with chili pastes.

Lime juice (fresh and herbal): Category 1 wines

Oyster sauce (savory and rich): Category 6 wines and wooded whites from Category 3

1 teaspoon curry powder in 1 cup yogurt (mildly spicy and light smoky): Category 2 wines and aromatic wines from Category 1

Curry paste (spicy and smoky): Category 3 and 7 wines

Ground chili paste (fiery and sweet): well-chilled fruity reds from Category 2 and also wines from Categories 4 and 5

We encourage you to try our flavor profile technique for yourself using these taste tests and the recipes that follow. Once you feel comfortable within our guidelines, you can start to explore wine pairing with more confidence and to develop your personal tastes. Please bear in mind that personal reactions to flavors and sensations will ultimately play a part in choosing any wine or food.

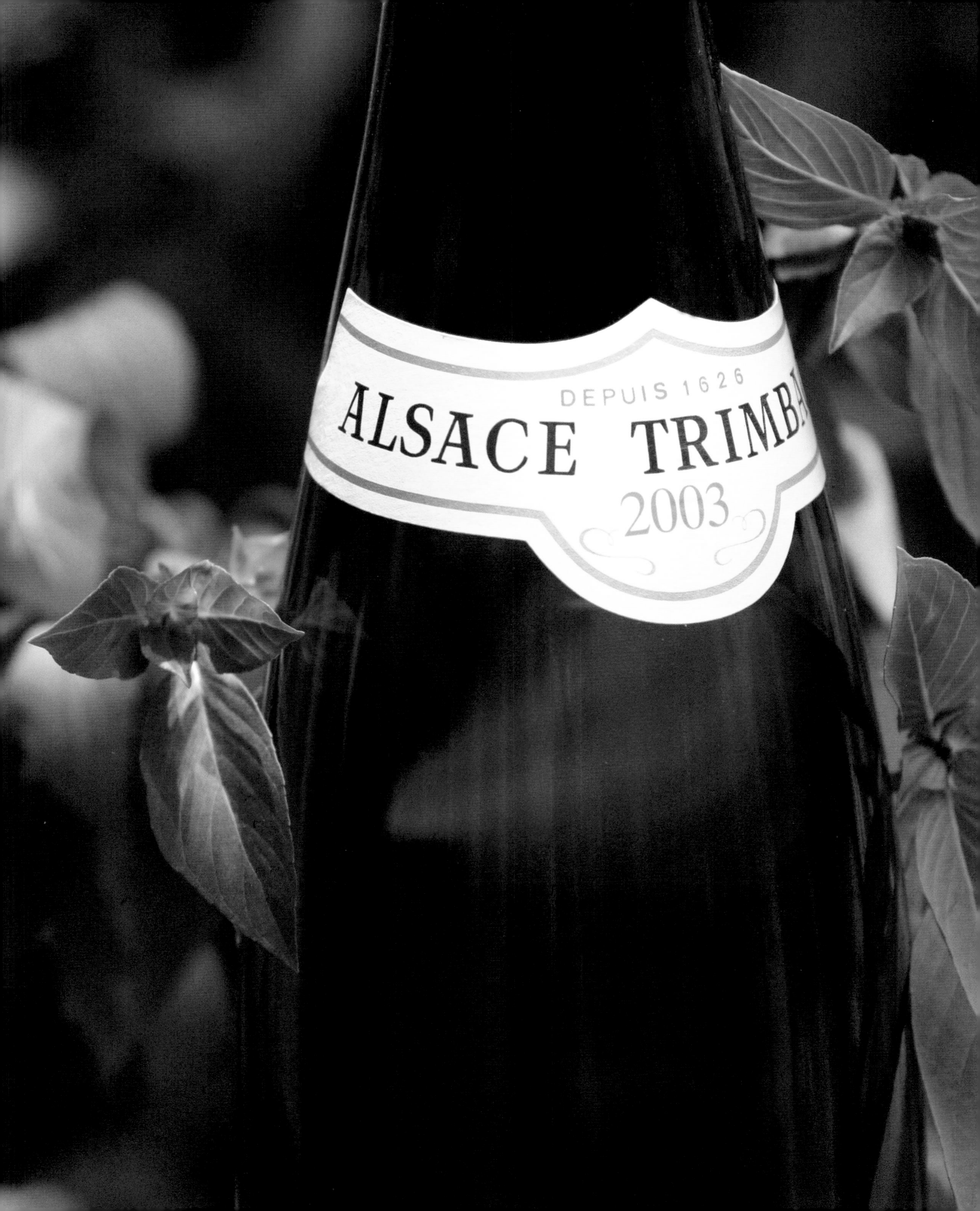
DEPUIS 1626
ALSACE TRIMB
2003

Fresh & Herbal Flavors

The hallmark of the recipes in this section is the fresh purity of their flavors. The primary herbs are basil, cilantro, lemongrass, and lime leaves. Cooking methods include boiling, steaming, and poaching, as well as serving raw ingredients with a variety of tart or salty condiments, such as fish sauces, vinegar, and lime juice.

We have listed specific wine suggestions for each recipe. However, you can match any of the wines in Category 1 with any of the recipes in this section. These wines share a similar taste profile. They are dry, tart, and clean the palate. They brighten the flavor of fishy, salty, oily, and fried food. Their tangy flavors also support those of fresh, zesty herbs and do not overpower delicate steamed or poached dishes.

Vietnam

GOI CUON
Shrimp Rolls

The Vietnamese often use rice paper (banh trang) for wrapping food parcels because it delicately encases the food without over-powering its flavors, as wheat-based wrappers would.

Dipping sauce
1 small red chili, thinly sliced
3$\frac{1}{4}$ tbsp sugar
2 cloves garlic, minced
2 tbsp finely shredded carrots
1 cup (225 ml) rice vinegar
2 tbsp lime juice
4 tbsp fish sauce (nam pla)
1 tbsp chopped peanuts

For rolls
7 oz (200 g) shrimp
7 oz (200 g) pork
2 oz (60 g) rice vermicelli
16 rice paper wrappers
$\frac{1}{2}$ cup leaf cilantro (coriander leaves)
$\frac{1}{4}$ cup mint leaves
$\frac{1}{4}$ cup basil leaves
1 medium-sized carrot, finely shredded
2 cups bean sprouts
1 large cucumber, finely shredded
2 cups shredded iceberg lettuce
1 cup minced scallions (green onions)

To make the dipping sauce, put all the sauce ingredients in a bowl and mix well to combine. Chill.

Trim the shrimp and cook them in boiling water. Remove the shells, cut along the tops to remove the black veins, and slice each shrimp lengthwise. Cook the pork in the boiling water and then mince coarsely. Soften the rice vermicelli by immersing it in boiling water for 2 to 3 minutes. Drain well.

Immerse a wrapper in a shallow plate of hot water for about 10 seconds to soften it. Spread it on a clean, dry towel, and then place some herbs (3 cilantro leaves, 2 mint leaves, and 1 basil leaf) on the bottom half of the wrapper. Pile a little of the vegetables and a small amount of the softened vermicelli on top of the leaves. Add some shrimp and pork. Fold in the sides of the wrapper and roll it up tightly into a cylinder.

Make more rolls till the ingredients are all used up. Cover the finished rolls with a damp tea towel and then wrap the parcel with plastic. Chill it for an hour before serving with the dipping sauce.

This dish's herbal flavors and the touch of sweetness that comes from the dipping sauce call for a wine with zippy acidity and well-defined fruit flavors to balance it.

OLD WORLD AND NEW WORLD
Dry sparkling wine, from the simple to the most complex.

ALTERNATIVES
The sweetness in the ingredients can be enhanced by choosing a wine that has a light touch of sweetness, such as an Austrian Grüner Veltliner or an off-dry Scheurebe from Rheinhessen. We also suggest a Sylvaner della Valle Isarco. Among the many top Italian producers, we like Hans Rottensteiner or Peter Plieger's Kuenhof Estate. These Sylvaners have fresh lemony fragrances and are infused with delicate mineral notes on the finish. The Sylvaners of Cave de Pfaffenheim, Domaine Dirler-Cade, and Dopff & Irion, of Alsace, France, can be served with confidence, as can the wines of Robert Gilliard (Switzerland) and Rudolf Fürst (Germany).

Australian Semillons and blends, some lightly oaked, are good alternatives. Reliable producers include Glenguin, Peter Lehmann, Penfolds "Rawson's Retreat Bin 21," Rosemount, St. Halett "Poachers Blend," Tyrells, and Tatachilla.

Citrusy unoaked Chardonnays from Australia make fine partners. The list of good producers is a veritable A-Z: Alkoomi, Basedow, Cassegrain, Delatite, Elderton, Goundrey, Moss Brothers, Poet's Corner, Salitage, Shaw and Smith, and Tulloch. You might even like to try wines made from Chenin Blanc, Colombard, and Verdelho. These grape varieties are grown in Europe and the New World.

China

CARAMELIZED SHRIMP

Stir frying and deep frying are classic Chinese cooking methods. These techniques allow vegetables to retain their crunchiness while meats and seafood remain tender. In Singapore and Malaysia, this double-cooked shrimp dish is known as Har Lok.

7 oz (200 g) shrimp, washed and trimmed with shells kept on
1 tsp salt
4 cloves garlic, minced
1 tbsp minced ginger
3 scallions (green onions), chopped coarsely
2 cups oil

Sauce
1 tsp cornstarch
2 tbsp soy sauce
2 tsp sugar
1 tbsp dry sherry
$1/4$ tsp five-spice powder
1 tbsp tomato ketchup

Rub the shrimp with the salt and let them stand for 10 minutes. Meanwhile, prepare the sauce by combining the sauce ingredients together with a fork.

Heat 2 cups of oil in a wok or a deep pan until the oil is smoking. Put the shrimp in carefully and deep fry over high heat until they are almost done. Ladle out the shrimp to drain on paper towels so they remain crisp.

Turn off the heat and remove all but 2 tablespoons of oil from the wok. Reheat the wok and when the oil begins to smoke, sauté the garlic and ginger until they are fragrant and golden. Now return the shrimp, include the sauce mixture, and fry until the shrimp are evenly well coated and caramelized.

Transfer into a serving dish, garnish with the scallions, and serve.

Dry, aromatic wines, particularly Rieslings, with their zesty palate-cleansing acidity, make excellent partners for this dish.

OLD WORLD
A dry Riesling from a German (such as Georg Breuer, Koehler-Rupprecht, or Emrich-Schonleber), Austrian (such as Bründlmayer, F. X. Pichler, Jurtschitsch, Hiedler, and Mittelbach-Tegernseerhof), or Alsace producer (André Ostertag, Spielmann, Trimbach, or Zind-Humbrecht).

NEW WORLD
Similar Riesling wines can be had from Fromm, Gibbston Valley, and Pegasus Bay (New Zealand), Crawford River, Frankland Estate, Grosset, and Houghton (Australia).

ALTERNATIVES
Try any Spanish Albariño. Dry sparkling rosés would also work well and add a charming dash of color. Lanson and Taittinger are favorite French houses offering "pink" Champagne. The Brut Rosés of Kristone (California) and Villiera (South Africa) are worth seeking out. Do not overlook the sweeter rosé styles, from Portugal's Mateus to California's sparkling White Zinfandels.

China

DEEP-FRIED GROUPER

Cutting, slicing, or scoring fish achieves a homogeneity of crispy texture. Frying a second time creates a super-crisp dish.

1 grouper or a firm, white-fleshed fish, approx. 1 lbs (500 g)
Cornstarch to coat fish
2 cloves garlic, minced
3 tsp minced ginger
1 1/4 cups (280 ml) clear vegetable stock
1 scallion (green onions), sliced
3 tbsp Chinese vinegar
2 tsp sesame oil
1 stalk leaf cilantro (coriander leaves), torn into sprigs
Oil for deep frying

Sauce
3 tsp cornstarch
1 tbsp light soy sauce
4 tbsp sugar
2 tsp sherry (optional)
1/4 tsp salt
3 tbsp vegetable stock

Clean and gut the fish. Make several diagonal deep cuts on both sides of the prepared fish and set aside.

To make the sauce, first put 3 teaspoons of cornstarch into 2 tablespoons of cold water and mix till a smooth consistency is achieved. Combine all the sauce ingredients with the prepared cornstarch mixture and set aside.

Put enough oil in a wok to immerse the whole fish. Heat the oil over a high heat (340°F/170°C). Meanwhile, wipe the fish dry and coat it lightly with cornstarch. When the oil is bubbling, slip the fish into the oil slowly, head first. The fish should be totally immersed. Deep fry for 3 minutes, then remove the fish. Reheat the oil and immerse the fish again to fry until it is golden. This double-frying technique makes the fish truly crisp, cooking it on the inside while keeping the outside from cooking too quickly. Remove the fish, draining away the excess oil, and arrange it on a serving platter.

Heat 1 teaspoon of oil and sauté the garlic and ginger till they are fragrant and golden. Pour in the vegetable stock and bring it to a boil. Add the prepared sauce mixture and stir until it has thickened. Include the scallions. Turn off the heat and stir in the vinegar and sesame oil.

Ladle the sauce over the fish and garnish with sprigs of leaf cilantro. Serve hot.

Serve any young, refreshingly fizzy sparkling wine with a light fragrance (not a Champagne, whose fragrance usually has more mineral and yeasty notes). The liveliness of a young sparkling wine complements the crispy texture of the skin of the fish. The wine's delicate aroma allows the flavor of the fish to come through.

OLD WORLD
Carpenè Malvolti Prosecco Cuvée Oro or a Bisol Garnéi Prosecco di Valdobbiadene. Both wines have clean floral bouquets that will not clash with the ginger and leaf cilantro as well as a zesty acidity that cuts through the fattiness of deep frying. You may also wish to try Cava (Spain), Crémant de Die (France), and even Sekt (Germany).

NEW WORLD
From California, options might be Domaine Carneros Brut or Gloria Ferrer Sonoma Brut; from Australia try Yellowglen; and from New Zealand, No.1 Family Estate. A slightly more exotic suggestion is a Vinedos San Marcos Brut (Mexico).

ALTERNATIVES
Try aromatic still wines, such as the Gewürztraminer Nussbaumer from the Cooperative at Tramin, Alto Adige in Italy, or the same varietal from Cave de Turckheim in Alsace, France. Try also a Picpoul from France's Languedoc region or a Vin de Savoie.

New World Gewürztraminers also work well with this dish. From California, Gewürztraminer often has a touch of sweetness. Good producers include Louis M. Martini, Firestone, Chateau St. Jean, Bouchaine, Thomas Fogarty, and Hursch. Dry lime- or lemon-flavored white wines are other options. Otherwise you will find suitable matches in wines such as Pinot Gris and Verdelho.

India

SPICED MUSSELS

India, which as recently as 1847 was a collection of some six hundred separate kingdoms, has a rich and complex culinary history that has spread its influence throughout the subcontinent to the countries of Pakistan, Nepal, Bhutan, Bangladesh, and Sri Lanka. If there is a unifying element in Indian cuisine, it is its subtle blending of spices. Garam masala (a blend that usually contains cumin, red pepper, fennel seeds, cardamom, and coriander seeds) is what gives this Anglo-Indian dish, inspired by English colonials, its Indian character.

1 lb (500 g) mussels, rinsed, and debearded
3 tbsp mayonnaise
1 tsp garam masala
$^1/_2$ red chili, deseeded and chopped finely
2 scallions (green onions), chopped finely
$^1/_4$ cup (45 g) white breadcrumbs
Salt

Bring 2 cups of water to a boil in a large pan. Put in the mussels, cover, and cook over high heat for 5 minutes. Discard any unopened mussels. Remove the meat from the opened shells and reserve the shells.

Chop the mussel meat finely and mix with the mayonnaise. Add the garam masala, chili, scallions, and breadcrumbs. Taste and adjust for salt, then spoon the mixture back into the shells and serve.

Sparkling wines are a traditional partner for simply prepared seafood: they enliven the food in the same way as a squeeze of lemon does.

OLD WORLD
India's famous sparkling wine, Omar Khayyam, would be a fine match, as would a fresh, crisp Orvieto from a producer like Castello della Sala or Barberani.

NEW WORLD
From the New World, try Felton Road or Milton Riesling (New Zealand), or Riesling from Grosset, Orlando's Steingarten, Annie's Lane, or Pikes (Australia).

ALTERNATIVES
Spanish Viuras (White Riojas) or dry Furmints from Hungary such as Oremus Tokaji Furmint Mandolas. Each of these grape varieties has fine acidity, and wines made from them, while creamy, have enough tang to harmonize with any lingering salty sensations from the seafood.

Californian pink and blush wines are yet another alternative. Try Bonny Doon Big House Pink or Toad Hollow Eye of the Toad.

Japan

SHRIMP TEMPURA

Tempura, derived from the Western practice of dipping foods into batter and deep frying them, is the legacy of mid-sixteenth century Portuguese traders and sailors who made their way to Japanese shores. Tempura is eaten hot, and its crispness is softened slightly by a quick dip in sauce.

10 large shrimp
Flour for coating shrimp
Oil for deep frying

Batter
1 cup (225 ml) iced water
$^1/_4$ cup (60 g) tempura flour or light cake flour
2 egg yolks

Dipping sauce
Bottled instant dashi granules (dashi-no-moto)
$^1/_4$ cup finely grated white radish (daikon), squeezed dry

Follow the instructions on the bottle to make the tempura dipping sauce. The sauce is served in individual bowls offered with a teaspoon of grated white radish in small plates on the side. The grated radish is added to the sauce at the table.

Shell and devein the shrimp, leaving the tails intact. Make shallow cuts on the underside and gently spread the cuts open, taking care not to break the shrimp. This is to prevent them from curling during cooking. Pat the shrimp dry with kitchen towels and lightly dredge with flour, leaving the tail uncoated. Set aside.

Heat the oil in a deep pan. Prepare the tempura batter while the oil is heating up. Beat the egg yolks lightly. Add the iced water and mix with a few strokes. Include the tempura flour and beat the mixture till the ingredients are loosely combined. This batter should be lumpy to achieve a light and crispy crust when deep frying. If the temperature of the water used to mix the flour is high or if the batter is mixed too thoroughly or vigorously, the result will be a soggy crust.

A substitute for tempura flour is cake or pastry flour, which has less gluten than regular flour. Techniques employed to suppress the formation of gluten include adding cold water, little by little, to the mixture and adding a pinch of baking powder.

Test the heat of the oil by dripping in a bit of batter. The oil is sufficiently hot when the batter sinks and rises to the surface with bubbles around its edges. Dip each shrimp into the batter, leaving the tail uncoated. Deep fry quickly in the hot oil. Remove when the crust is pale golden and drain on paper towels. Serve at once.

When the food is crispy and batter-fried, think zippy, palate-cleansing acidity for the wine. The sweetness of the shrimp allows you to serve complex sparkling wines.

OLD WORLD
Rosé Champagne-Billecart-Salmon, Gosset and Veuve Clicquot are personal favorites. Otherwise, try an elegant Franciacorta from Bellavista, Ca' del Bosco or Villa.

NEW WORLD
New World sparkling wines are every bit as crisp and appealing as their European counterparts. From California, try a Brut style from Iron Horse, Jordan, Roederer, and Schramsberg. From Australia, look for Domaine Chandon, Green Point, Seaview, or Seppelts.

ALTERNATIVES
If you are not looking for such a high-flying match, any good crisp white will do. At the top of the list would be a French Loire Valley Muscadet de Sèvre et Maine (from any producer and without the phrase *sur lie* on the label) or a Soave DOC (Denominazione di origine controllata). Others to try are any Austrian Grüner Veltliner, Xarello blends from Catalonia, Spain, or Vinho Verde from Portugal.

New Zealand excels in bright, crisp whites. Why not try a zesty Riesling from Martinborough Vineyards or Corbans? South African Chenin Blancs sometimes have a more viscous texture, which reacts well with deep-fried mushrooms and other vegetables such as okra, radish, and onion.

China

CANTONESE
STEAMED SNAPPER

The province of Canton has a semitropical climate that allows for year-round crops of rice, fruit, and vegetables, while the province's long coastline provides a rich fishing ground in the South China Sea. Since the Cantonese enjoy such abundance, they insist on the absolute freshness of cooking ingredients and have become connoisseurs of flavor and texture. The primary cooking methods in this region – steaming, poaching, and stir frying – emphasize and enhance the natural flavors of the main ingredients.

1 snapper, 1 $^1/_2$ lbs (700 g), cleaned and scaled
1 scallion (spring onion), shredded
1 tbsp finely sliced ginger
2 tsp white Chinese rice wine
2 tbsp soy sauce
1 tsp sesame oil
1 stalk leaf cilantro (coriander leaves), torn into sprigs
White pepper

Wash and pat the fish dry. Place the shredded scallion into a heatproof serving dish and then place the fish on top. Marinate the fish with the ginger, Chinese rice wine, soy sauce, and sesame oil, and leave to stand for 30 minutes.

Prepare a steamer or a large wok for steaming. If you are using a wok, place a cake tin or steaming stand in the wok to support the dish of fish. Pour in enough water to bring the water level to 2 inches (5 cm) beneath the top of the cake tin or stand.

Bring the water to a boil. Place the dish containing the marinated fish on the support. Cover and steam over high heat for 10 minutes. The fish is done when its eyes turn white and begin to bulge. Remove the dish, garnish with the leaf cilantro, and, finally, add the white pepper to taste. Serve hot.

The secret of this dish is the cooking time. This, of course, will vary with the size of the fish, so adjust accordingly.

A dry white or rosé wine that echoes the freshness of the cilantro and spring onion.

OLD WORLD
A dry rosé from Italy, a Bardolino Chiaretto from Corte Gardoni or Cavalchina. From France, a Rosé de Loire from Domaine des Trottieres, a Chateau Gravette Rosé of Minervois or Balland Sancerre Rosé (France). We also like the Anjou Rosés of Mark Angeli and V & V Lebreton, although any Rosé d'Anjou will be fine.

NEW WORLD
From California, try a fresh and fruity Sauvignon Blanc from Dunnewood Vineyards, Grgich Hills, St. Supery, Parducci, or Wente Vineyards Selection. From New Zealand, Chile, or Australia, any unwooded Chardonnay will make a good match.

ALTERNATIVES
The fragrances of a crisp, dry wine made from aromatic grape varieties (Gewürztraminer, Muscat, Riesling) will add a dimension of enjoyment to this simple dish. Pacific Rim Dry Riesling from California's Boony Doon winery would be ideal. Also try dry German wines such as Johannes Leitz (Riesling Rüdesheimer Berg Schlossberg) or Austria's Loimer (Riesling Lagenloiser Steinmassl). The Müller-Thurgau-Gewürztraminer blend called Palava by Pezinok (Slovak) and Velke Bilovice Sauvignon (Czech) fit here too.

You can also venture a Sauvignon Blanc from a top Friuli Venezia Giulia producer. Among the many, Vie di Romans, Beltrame, and Livio Felluga stand out. Also good is a Sauvignon Blanc from New Zealand. Good names to look for are Cloudy Bay, Forrest Estate, Babich, Hunter's, Marlborough, and Wither Hills.

Laos and Thailand

LAAP
Chicken Salad

Laap is a distinctive Laotian dish that has been adopted by the Thais. Traditional laap contains chopped raw fish or meat: chicken, duck, pork, beef, buffalo, or game. This is a cooked version, dressed with onion, chilies, and mint. The bright, zesty flavoring of limes (juice, zest, and leaves) adds a sprightly quality to this salad.

1 $^1/_2$ lbs (700 g) chicken breast
1 tbsp oil
4 shallots, thinly sliced
1 stalk lemongrass
2 cloves garlic, minced
$^1/_2$ tsp pepper
1 tsp fish sauce (nam pla)
1 tsp lime juice
1 tsp salt
3 red chilies, sliced
1 head of lettuce, leaves separated, rinsed, and dried
$^1/_4$ cup (60 g) mint leaves
1 cucumber, skinned and cut into 2-inch (5-cm) pieces
1 carrot, skinned and cut into 2-inch (5-cm) pieces
3 runner beans, deveined and cut into 2-inch (5-cm) pieces
2 stalks scallions (green onions), cut into 2-inch (5-cm) pieces

Debone and skin the chicken and remove any cartilage, then cut the breasts into bite-sized pieces. Heat some water in a pot and boil the chicken pieces until they are cooked. Remove and mince.

Heat 1 tablespoon of oil in a wok or deep pan. Sauté the shallots till they become transparent. Add the chicken and keep stirring, separating the minced meat to prevent clumping. The mince is ready when it is slightly browned and evenly coated. Set aside.

Cut off the white stem of the lemongrass and discard the leaves. Trim off the root end and slice the white stem into rounds. Put the garlic, lemongrass, pepper, fish sauce, lime juice, and salt into a food processor and grind into a coarse paste. Add this mixture to the cooked chicken and combine it with the sliced chilies. Toss well.

Serve the mince mixture with lettuce, mint, cucumber, carrots, runner beans, and scallions on the side.

Lime juice, mint, lemongrass, and scallions are all fresh, green flavors that call for an aromatic white wine with similar characteristics.

OLD WORLD
Try a dry Gewürztraminer from Italy's Alto Adige. Hans Rottensteiner and the Cantina Produttori Santa Maddalena are two good ones. If you are looking for something a little bubbly from France, you could select Domaine de l'Aigle Crémant de Limoux or any Crémant de Loire. The choice of style – brut (dry) or demi-sec (lightly sweet) – depends on your palate since both will work with this dish.

NEW WORLD
A Sauvignon Blanc from Australia (top producers include Bridgewater Mill, Geoff Weaver, and Nepenthe) and even New Zealand's Hunter's, Neudorf, and Seresin would underscore the flavor and fragrance of the herbs, lift the subtle flavor of the chicken, and clean the palate.

An affordable New Zealand Sauvignon Blanc is Monkey Bay.

ALTERNATIVES
Try the Chenin Blancs from South Africa, which come in dry and sweet versions. Reliable producers include Beaumont, Ken Forrester, L'Avenir, Leopard's Leap, Mulderbosch, and Nederburg. Sauvignon Blancs from Chile, such as those produced by Casa Lapostolle, Los Boldos, and Villard, are also good partners. The Japanese Chateau Mercian, and Aruga Branca's Koshu make a statement here.

Thailand

THOT MAN PLA
Fish Cakes

There are certain bright, zesty flavorings that set Thai food apart from other Asian cuisines. Among these are limes, basil, and sweet aromatic shallots. Instead of making red curry paste (see page 114), you can use the packaged version.

2 lbs (1 kg) fish fillets cut into chunks, deboned, and skinned
1 tsp salt
$^1/_2$ tsp pepper
$^1/_3$ cup (80 ml) red curry paste
3 eggs, lightly beaten
2 tbsp fish sauce (nam pla)
1 cup finely chopped green beans (optional)
2 kaffir lime leaves (limau purut)
    or 2 basil leaves, finely chopped
Oil for frying

Cucumber salad
1 cucumber, sliced
6 shallots, chopped
1 red chili, chopped
2 tbsp sugar
1 tbsp vinegar
1 tsp salt
$^1/_2$ cup (250 ml) hot water

Combine the fish, salt, pepper, red curry paste, eggs, and fish sauce. Use the mixture to make balls of about $1^1/_2$ inches (4 cm) in diameter and fold the kaffir lime leaves and green beans, if using, into the balls. Flatten each ball into a patty. Repeat with the remaining ingredients.

Heat 5 tablespoons of oil in a wok or deep pan over medium heat. When the oil is hot, fry the fish cakes until they turn golden brown. Drain on a paper towel.

To make the cucumber salad, arrange the cucumber, shallots, and chili in layers in a serving bowl. In a separate bowl, make a dressing by combining the sugar, vinegar, salt, and hot water. Stir until the sugar has dissolved. Pour the dressing over the salad and serve with the fish cakes.

A wine with a lightly mineral vein is a good match for these fish cakes. It should reflect the salinity of the fish sauce.

OLD WORLD
Try any of the many reliable dry Semillon-Sauvignon Blanc blends from France's Bordeaux region, especially the white Graves and Pessac Léognans. Australia, too, offers good versions of Semillon and blends based on that grape variety. Top producers include Tyrells, McWilliams, Yalumba, and Hungerford Hill.

ALTERNATIVES
Wines made from white Italian varieties, especially Falanghina, whose light vein of salinity merges well with the rich salinity of the fish sauce. Among the many good producers are Villa Matilde and Di Majo Norante.

Try any good, firmly structured dry rosé. An Italian favorite is Cirò Rosato from the Calabrian producer Librandi.

New Zealand produces some very attractive rosés. Good examples are Stoneleigh Pinot Rosé, Esk Valley Black Label, and Kirkpatrick Estate Wild Rosé. Producers of excellent California rosé and blush wines include Ironstone, Burlwood Cellars, and Napa Ridge.

Another good match would be a Friulano from Italy. This food-friendly white has the ability to go well with practically any fish or fresh herb-seasoned dish. It is the special wine of the region, so most Friulian producers make good ones.

For something different, try a sweet French wine that mirrors the Thai sweet chili sauce: Domaine Cauhape Petit Manseng, a Jurançon, or Domaine des Baumard Quarts de Chaume.

Cambodia

NHUEM SALAD

There are various versions of this Cambodian salad. Some include shredded meat; others feature only vegetables. We like the one with noodles because it makes for a light meal for one person or starters for four persons.

4 cloves garlic, peeled and thinly sliced
3 cups finely shredded cabbage
$^1/_2$ lb (230 g) cellophane noodles (rice noodles)
I cup bean sprouts
I small onion, thinly sliced
I carrot, shredded
I green bell pepper, cored, seeded, and sliced into rings
5 basil leaves, finely shredded
5 fresh mint leaves, finely shredded
I sprig leaf cilantro (coriander leaves)
I tbsp oil for frying

Salad dressing
6 tbsp fish sauce (nam pla)
4 tbsp lime juice
I tbsp water
4 tsp sugar
3 cloves garlic, chopped finely
I bird's eye chili, chopped finely
3 tbsp dry-roasted peanuts, chopped finely
Salt and freshly ground black pepper to taste

Mix the ingredients for the salad dressing together and set aside.

Heat the oil in a wok or deep pan. When the oil is smoking hot, sauté the garlic for about 30 seconds. The moment the garlic slices turn golden brown, remove them or they will burn. Set aside on paper towels to soak up the oil.

Blanch the cellophane rice noodles in boiling water until they are cooked but not soggy. Remove, plunge in cold water, and drain in a colander. Blanch the bean sprouts in the same water for 30 seconds, then remove, drain, and rinse with cold water.

Combine the cabbage, noodles, bean sprouts, onion, carrot, bell peppers, basil, mint, cilantro, and fried garlic in a salad bowl.

Pour on the dressing. Toss and serve.

A wine with fresh acidity will play off the saltiness of the fish sauce and the herbal flavors while contrasting with the crunchy texture of the salad.

OLD WORLD
Chablis from Domaine Laroche or La Chablisienne, or a Sauvignon de Touraine (all French).

NEW WORLD
Try the Sauvignon Blancs of Cakebread, Honig, Shooting Star, and Mirasou (from California) and a Vinho Verde (Portugal). All these wines combine a creamy fruitiness with tangy zest.

ALTERNATIVES
A Marco de Bartoli Zibbibo Secco, with its pure grapeyness, is an interesting partner. It adds an attractive richness to the peanuts in the dressing. A Carema (a Nebbiolo-based red wine from Piedmont) has an appealing fresh fruitiness that underscores the interesting blend of flavors in this dish: fish sauce and chili. Reliable producers include: Ferrando, Cantina dei Produttori di Carema, and Orsolani. Italy also has good whites that fill the bill. Grape varieties to look for include Greco, Insolia, and Trebbiano.

From France, the grapefruit-apricot aromas of Michel Fonne's Domaine René Barth Pinot Gris make an excellent match. Although the flavors are rich, the taste has an edge that cleanses the palate. A lightly floral Italian Soave DOC, an Entre-Deux-Mers (from any producer in this Bordeaux region) or an Australian Semillon (all are dry, tangy, and refreshing palate cleansers) are also good matches. Also suitable are Californian Pinot Blancs from Chalone or Mirrasou, the Pinot Blanc of Elk Cove, and the blended Pinot Gris-Riesling-Gewurztraminer called Brooks "Amycas" (both from Oregon).

Singapore/Malaysia

SQUID SALAD

This is an attractive and easy-to-prepare dish with strong Asian flavors. It can be served either hot or cold.

1¼ lb (600 g) squid
1 cup bean sprouts
½ cucumber
1 tomato
2 egg whites, lightly beaten
2 cups oil
1 stalk leaf cilantro (coriander leaves), torn into sprigs

Seasoned flour
1 tsp Szechuan pepper
1 tsp white pepper
1 tsp black pepper
½ cup (60 g) plain flour
¼ cup (45 g) rice flour
2 tsp salt

Salad dressing
1 tbsp sherry
2 tbsp soy sauce
1 tsp Chinese black vinegar
1 tbsp minced ginger
2 cloves garlic, minced
2 scallions (spring onions), thinly sliced
1 tsp sweet chili sauce

Combine the ingredients for the salad dressing in a small bowl and set aside. Rinse the vegetables and cut the cucumber and tomato into thin slices. Arrange the salad on a serving platter and chill.

Open the squid hoods, wash thoroughly, and pat them dry. Cut the squid into 1 x 1½ inch (2.5 x 4 cm) pieces, and score a diamond pattern on them.

Combine the ingredients for the seasoned flour in a bowl.

Heat the oil in a wok or deep pan. Test the heat of the oil by dropping in a cube of bread. The oil is sufficiently hot when the bread browns in 15 seconds. Dip the pieces of squid in the egg white and then coat them well with the seasoned flour. Deep fry small batches for about 1 minute or until they are lightly golden and cooked through. Drain on a paper towel and season with a pinch of salt. Toss the salad with the dressing, arrange the squid on top, and garnish with the cilantro leaves. Serve.

Note: To make this a one-dish meal, cook some cellophane noodles, chill, and add to the salad.

While sparkling wines are a natural match for this deep-fried dish, serve any light dry, wine. You will find that its acidity will highlight the flavors of the dish, and its gentle fruitiness will provide a canvas on which the taste of the squid and of the multiflavored dressing will be brought into sharp relief.

OLD WORLD
Frascati, with its lively freshness and supple flavor, makes a fine backdrop for this dish. There are many good producers. Try one from Fontana Candida or Castel De Paolis. A Swiss Chasselas from D'Auvernier, with its mineral, fresh apple, and musky melon flavors, or the floral nuanced example from Boxler; an Albariño from Lusco do Miño (Spain); or a sprightly Vinho Verde from Portugal all have that bracing cleansing effect on the palate that really enhances grilled and fried seafood.

NEW WORLD
Again, a Sauvignon Blanc from New Zealand or California would be an interesting match. New Zealand excels with this variety, and any producer will be likely to produce a good-quality wine. In California good producers include (in addition to those already mentioned) Markham, Stonegate, and the Ernest & Julio Gallo Twin Valley range.

ALTERNATIVES
Saumur Brut from France's Loire region, Spanish Cava, German Sekt, Italian dry Spumante, or any New World sparkling wine. Try also the Semillons from Washington state. Among the top producers are Hogue, Goodsport, and Blackwood Canyon.

Savory & Rich Flavors

The primary herbs and seasonings are star anise, roasted coriander seeds, cinnamon, and cardamom. Sauces include barbecue sauce, sweet soy sauce, mushroom sauce, and general nut-based sauces. These recipes usually feature meat or meaty mushrooms. The cooking methods include roasting, barbecuing, stewing, grilling, broiling, heavy smoking, and charring.

We have listed specific wine suggestions for each recipe. However, you can match any of the chewy high-tannin reds from Category 6 successfully with any of the recipes in this section. The tannins in the wine combine with the proteins and fats in the food to create a rich, round, satisfying flavor.

India
ROGAN JOSH
Lamb Casserole

Verdant and mountainous Kashmir, India's most northerly state, shares a border with China. Its subtly spiced cuisine is a legacy of its former Mogul rulers, who favored rich and creamy dishes that frequently contained almonds or cashews. Saffron, chilies, and ginger are among Kashmir's signature spices.

8 lamb shanks, approx. 1$^3/_4$ lbs (800 g)
3 cloves
5 cardamoms
1-inch (2.5-cm) piece of ginger, ground into a paste
5 cloves garlic, ground into a paste
Salt to taste
$^1/_4$ cup (55 ml) yogurt
1 onion, chopped and ground into a paste, then browned
    in a little oil
1 tsp chili powder
2 cups (450 ml) stock
$^1/_4$ cup (55 ml) tomato purée
1 tbsp almonds, crushed into a paste
$^1/_2$ tsp garam masala
Oil for cooking

Garnish
1-inch (2.5-cm) piece of ginger, julienned
1 sprig leaf cilantro (coriander leaves)
A pinch of saffron threads, soaked in 3 tbsp rose water
    or hot water

Heat 1 tablespoon of oil in a frying pan over a medium heat. When the oil is smoking, sauté the cloves and cardamoms till they crackle. Add the ginger and garlic pastes and cook until almost dry. Add the lamb shanks, salt, yogurt, browned onion paste and chili powder. Stir for 5 minutes and raise the heat to high. Add the stock, and, when boiling, turn down the heat and simmer until the meat is tender. This should take about 30 minutes.

Remove the lamb shanks and place them in an oven-proof casserole. Strain the curry from the original frying pan into another pan. To this, add the tomato puree and cook over a high heat until the liquid is reduced by half. Stir in the almond paste and the garam masala. Pour the mixture over the shanks. Garnish, then cover the casserole, and cook for 10 minutes in a hot oven (375° F/190°C). Serve.

Any well-structured red wine from Category 6 will enhance the meat and be made more mellow by the yogurt. The wine's fruit will enfold the spices.

OLD WORLD
Any blend of Sangiovese and Cabernet from a good Tuscan producer will work very well. We particularly like the Girifalco produced by La Calonica. It offers a lively acidity, a sprinkling of black pepper, and a bright raspberry note on the palate that enhances the meld of creamy, sweet-savory flavors of this dish.

French reds from the Côte Rôtie (Château d'Ampuis, René Rostaing, and Gerin); Cahors (Triguedina or Lagrezette); and Bandol (Domaine Tempier, Château Pradeaux, and Château de Pibarnon) also fit in well, given their robust flavors.

NEW WORLD
Malbec-based wines from Argentina, such as those from Altavista, Altos de Medrano, Catena Zapata, Norton, Trapiche, Vina Patagonia, Vinas du Tupungato, and Weinert have juicy red fruit and hints of coffee and cinnamon. The fruit and spice marry well with the taste of this dish. California produces some great Sangioveses. Try one from Adler Fels, Benessere, Chameleon, Cosentino, or Dover Canyon.

ALTERNATIVES
Viña Orvalaiz Rosé (Spain) or Barberas from California or Texas make good alternatives.

India

BEEF KEBABS

The sprawling city of Delhi, India's capital, draws its 10 million inhabitants from all over the country, and its cuisine reflects this diversity of origin. Delhi, however, is particularly noted for its Mogul dishes and for its biryani cooked in clay pots, its ghee-enriched pilaus, and its kebabs.

9 oz (250 g) beefsteak
4 tbsp yogurt
2 tbsp lemon juice
1-inch (2.5-cm) piece of ginger, grated
1 clove garlic, crushed
1 tsp ground cumin
$^{1}/_{2}$ tsp ground coriander
$^{1}/_{4}$ tsp chili powder
1 tsp salt
Oil

Cut the meat into 2-inch (5-cm) cubes and marinate it with a mixture of the yogurt, lemon juice, ginger, garlic, cumin, coriander, chili powder, and salt. Cover and refrigerate for 12 hours, turning the meat regularly so it is well marinated.

Thread the meat onto metal skewers and broil under a hot flame. This enables you to collect the juices with a pan so that you can brush the meat while it is cooking. When the meat is done to your liking, remove and serve.

Beef and Category 6 red wines make a classic match. This is so even when the flavors are augmented by spices. The fruit in the wine makes the flavor liaison, while the tannin binds with the protein in the meat.

OLD WORLD
Aglianico-based wines – Di Majo Norante and Paternoster are top producers – make an excellent foil for this dish because they have the necessary richness and good crisp acidity to enhance both the beef and the spiced-yogurt marinade. Any good Bordeaux Supérieur or Cru Bourgeois would also work well.

NEW WORLD
Cabernet Sauvignon from the New World would also match. Try Vasse Felix, Cape Mentelle, Cullen, and Moss Wood, which are all from the Margaret River in Australia.

ALTERNATIVES
Rich, ripe Zinfandels from California: Alderbrook, Banister, Potelle, Gary Farell, Kenwood, Marietta, Mazzocco, Montevina, Ravenswood, Renwood, and Sobon, can handle the spice and broiled taste of the meat. If you prefer a white wine, experiment with oaked Chardonnays from Chile, Australia, or California.

BRAISED MUSHROOMS AND MUSTARD GREENS

Braising is a popular Chinese cooking method. In this recipe it brings out the rich meatiness of the mushrooms. Watercress and spinach are other vegetables suitable for this dish.

4 oz (115 g) dried Chinese mushrooms
1.6 oz (40 g) mustard greens (kailan)
3 cups hot water
2 tbsp dark soy sauce
2 tbsp sugar
1 tbsp sesame oil
3 tbsp cooking oil
1 clove garlic, minced

Bring a pot of water to a boil and blanch the mustard greens for 2 minutes. Remove and set aside.

Wash the mushrooms and then rehydrate them in the hot water for 20 minutes. Reserve this water. Remove the mushroom stems and discard them. Squeeze the water from the mushrooms into the water in which the mushrooms were soaked. Decant $1^1/_2$ cups (350 ml) of this liquid and add to it the dark soy sauce, sugar, and sesame oil to make a sauce.

Heat 3 tablespoons of cooking oil in a wok or deep pan. When the oil is smoking hot, sauté the garlic until it is fragrant. Put the mushrooms in the pan and then the sauce. When the liquid is bubbling, turn down the heat to simmer the mushrooms for about 30 minutes. Then add the mustard greens and continue cooking for 2 minutes.

When the vegetables take on a shiny appearance, put them onto a serving platter. Arrange the mushrooms, cap side up, on top of the mustard greens. Ladle the sauce over and serve.

These mushrooms are surprisingly "meaty" and call for a rich red from Category 6. The umami of the mushrooms encourages a merging of flavors, and the wine ultimately frames the dish.

OLD WORLD
A Syrah from the Tuscan Cortona area of Italy would make an excellent partner. A top wine is Il Bosco from d'Alessandro, whose Syrah is filled with dark spices (nutmeg and black pepper) and has a zesty grapefruit acidity. From France, consider the Rhône's Gigondas wines (Montmirail, St. Gayan, Tardieu-Laurent, and Vidal-Fleury).

NEW WORLD
Try Australian Shiraz (McWilliams, Seppelts, Bowen, Wynns, Rockfords, St. Halletts, Grant Burge, Chateau Reynella, Mitchells, Warrenmang and Wendouree) and Chilean Carmenère (Caliterra, Carmen, Concha y Toro, Luis Filepe Edwards, Gracia, and Los Robles). They all have suggestions of raspberry jam, with dark chocolate or spicy notes, and their sweet-savory flavors are allied with rich textures.

ALTERNATIVES
Try any fruity Pinot Noir.

Singapore

HOKKIEN FRIED NOODLES

This truly Singaporean noodle dish is also known as Rochor Noodles, named for the area where the dish first evolved. Rochor Road was close to the seaside markets that offered the freshest of seafood. So this braised-noodle dish is characterized by seafood stock, fresh shrimp, and squid rings.

1 lb (500 g) fresh yellow wheat noodles
3.2 oz (100 g) bean sprouts
8 oz (250 g) small shrimp
8 oz (250 g) squid
8 oz (250 g) roasted belly pork
1 tbsp cooking oil
1 cup (250 ml) water
2 tsp chopped garlic
2 tsp finely grated ginger
2 tsp soybean paste
2 tbsp soy sauce
2 stalks scallions (green onions), cut into 2-inch lengths

Prepare a pot of boiling water and blanch the noodles for 2 minutes. Remove them and allow to drain in a colander. Pinch off the roots of the bean sprouts.

Shell the shrimp, keeping the shells and heads to make a stock. Devein the shrimp. Clean the squid by cutting off the tentacles and removing the ink sac and beak. Wash thoroughly, cut the body into rings, and cut the tentacles into two pieces. Cut the roasted belly pork into strips.

To make the stock, heat a tablespoon of oil in a wok or deep pan over high heat. Sauté the shells and heads of the shrimp until they turn red, and then add a cup of water and bring to a boil. Lower the heat and simmer for 5 minutes. Strain the stock and reserve.

Heat 2 tablespoons of oil in a wok and sauté the ginger and garlic till they turn golden. Add the bean paste and pork and sauté for about 1 minute. Add the stock and soy sauce to this, then the shrimp and bean sprouts. Bring to a boil and add the noodles and scallions. Cover the wok and simmer over very low heat for 2 minutes, turning the noodles occasionally to prevent sticking. When the noodles have absorbed the stock and are soft but not mushy, the dish is ready.

When roasted pork is stir fried, it takes on a gamey, smoky taste. This element combines with the dark richness of the soy paste to create a dish well suited to a fresh yet elegant and well-balanced red wine from Category 6, which should, however, not be so rich as to overwhelm the nuances of the seafood.

OLD WORLD
This dish works very well with a Petra Toscana IGT (*Indicazione geografica tipica*) (the wine and the winery are both called Petra) that blends Merlot and Cabernet Sauvignon. We would also recommend any good AOC (*appellation d'origine contrôlée*) Bordeaux. Some good producers of this wine are Beau Rivage, Belle Garde, Commanderie de Queyret, and Roquefort. Bordeaux Supérieur wines include Chateau Naudonnet, Chateau Plaisance, Chateau Pierrail, Chateau de Seguin, and Tour de Mirambeau.

NEW WORLD
Merlot and its blends with other varieties are the order of the day here too. Producers include Beringer, Shafer and Clos du Bois (California); Columbia Crest and Andrew Hill (Washington); Casa Lapostolle and Santa Rita (Chile); and Katnook Estate and Yarra Yering (Australia). You might even find New World-styled Merlot-based wines from France, such as those from La Baume and Baron Philippe de Rothschild 's Vin de Pays.

ALTERNATIVES
Crisp Category 1 wines serve as a refreshing palate-cleanser. Try also sparking wines and rosé wines.

India

KORMA

This meat dish, cooked with pure ghee, is a basic recipe of Islamic Mogul cuisine. A mild curry, it became popular among the colonials during the days of the British Raj. Today, it has evolved into many different forms, employing yogurt and a spectrum of spices.

1 lb (500 g) lean lamb, beef, or chicken
1 tsp minced ginger
$^1/_4$ tsp salt
$9^1/_2$ oz (300 ml) yogurt
$^1/_2$ tsp cinnamon powder
1 tsp coriander powder
2 cardamoms, crushed
1 large onion, chopped
2 cloves garlic, crushed
2 tbsp ghee
2 tsp turmeric powder
Pinch of garam masala
Leaf cilantro (coriander leaves)

Cut the meat into 1-inch (2.5-cm) cubes and rub thoroughly with the minced ginger and salt. Combine the yogurt with the cinnamon, coriander, and cardamom. Marinate the meat with this mixture and allow it to stand overnight.

The following day, sauté the onion and the garlic in 2 tablespoons of ghee until they are tender. Stir in the turmeric and cook for 2 minutes. Add the meat and all the marinade. Cover and cook over low heat for about 1 hour or until the meat is tender. Sprinkle with garam masala and chopped cilantro. Serve.

Many Indians love to serve this dish with a tannic but fruity New World red. The tannins are softened by the yogurt, in the same way that they complement a creamy brie, and the broad fruit flavors blend well with the korma spices. Such wines from Category 6 include Australian Shiraz, Chilean Cabernet Sauvignon, and Spanish Tempranillo blends from Ribera del Duero or Rioja.

OLD WORLD
We recommend an oaked Barbera. Among the many good producers are Bava, Braida, La Ghersa, Elio Altare, and Prunotto.

NEW WORLD
California also produces some fine wines made with the Barbera grape.

ALTERNATIVES
Try New Wave Portuguese red wines such as Bela Fonte Baga, Quinta da Lagoalva, Quinta de Abrigada, Quinta das Maias, Fundacao Eugenio de Almeida, and Herdade do Esporão.

We also tried and liked Aquila Cabernet (Australia), Trapiche Malbec (Argentina), Viader "Dare" (California), and Abadia Retuerta Cuvée El Palomar (Spain).

Japan

YAKITORI

Yakitori is a compound word from *yaki*, meaning "grill," and *tori*, for "bird." It is simply a chicken kebab with variations using different chicken parts and innards. This dish is popular with "salarymen" – Japanese businessmen – when they meet after work.

2 chicken breasts, cut into bite-sized pieces
2 leeks, cut into 1-inch (2.5-cm) lengths
Salt
Bamboo skewers, soaked in water for about 6 hours

Marinade
4 tbsp mirin (Japanese rice wine)
3 tbsp dark soy sauce
1 tbsp miso paste (soy bean paste)
1 tbsp sesame oil
1 tbsp white vinegar
1 tbsp dark brown sugar

Combine all the ingredients for the marinade and stir until the sugar is dissolved. Marinate the chicken in this mixture overnight.

Skewer the chicken pieces alternating with the leeks. Grill them over a hot barbeque, using the remaining marinade as a glaze. Just before serving, sprinkle some salt on the meat.

The dense, sweetish sauce, which adds a layer of flavor to the smoky grilled chicken, calls for a velvety, plummy red from Category 6. The smoothness of the red mirrors the richness of the coating.

OLD WORLD
A particular favorite is a Salento IGT from Li Velli, but any well-made Negroamaro-based wine would work well. Bulgaria also produces good round reds: Domaine Boyar, Haskovo and Vini. Try also a Barbaresco from any of the many fine producers. Particular favorites are Ceretto, Bruno Giacosa, Michele Chiarlo, and Angelo Negro and Roagna.

NEW WORLD
Try Grenache from Jacob's Creek, Tim Adams, Charles Cimiky, Charles Melton, and Tatachilla (Australia).

ALTERNATIVES
Try rosé sparkling wines such as Cristalino Cava (Spain), Gloria Ferrer (California), and the Champagnes of Bruno Paillard, Laurent Perrier, and Billecart Salmon. The tarter wines will mirror the salty element, while fruity sparkling wines will bond with the tastes of the sweetish grilled meat. Fruity reds made from Cabernet Franc (particularly from France's Loire valley) work well. Also try Pinot Noirs such as Mud House, Perigrine, Quartz Reef, and Villa Maria (New Zealand).

China

STIR-FRIED BEEF WITH PEPPERS

This dish and its variations are standard offerings in Chinese restaurants all over the world. In northern China, ginger is often used to add a tingle to beef dishes.

14 oz (400 g) round or fillet steak
1 tsp corn flour
2 tbsp soy sauce
Pinch of pepper
1 onion, quartered
1 garlic clove, crushed
10 slices ginger

Sauce
3 tbsp soy sauce
1 tbsp oyster sauce or black bean paste
1 tbsp sherry
2 tsp sugar
1 tsp black pepper
1 tbsp tomato sauce
1 tsp sesame oil

2 tbsp corn flour rendered in $^1/_2$ cup (115 ml)
   cold water till smooth
$^1/_2$ green pepper, sliced
$^1/_2$ red pepper, sliced
6 tbsp cooking oil

Cut the beef along the grain into 2-inch (5-cm) strips. Mix together the corn flour, soy sauce, and pepper and use this to marinate the beef. Cover and refrigerate the meat for 30 minutes. Meanwhile, combine the sauce ingredients and set aside.

Heat 6 tablespoons of cooking oil in a wok or a deep pan. Brown the garlic and the ginger and stir fry the beef till just brown but not done. Remove the beef with a slotted spoon and set aside. Put in the onions and stir fry for 3 minutes till tender.

Combine the sauce mixture and peppers and cook for 1 minute, stirring constantly. Add the corn flour mixture and cook, stirring until the sauce has thickened. Finally, add the beef and stir fry for a minute or till the meat is just done. Serve immediately.

This is another match that plays on the natural affinity between beef and red wines. Red wines with chewy tannins from Category 6 such as Sagrantino, oaked Barbera, Barbaresco, and Barolo have a place here. So do wines based on Merlot, Tempranillo, and Shiraz. They all have the backbone to work well with this dish, and they can handle the sprinkling of ginger while enhancing the beef.

OLD WORLD
A particular favorite is Gran Reserva Rioja.

NEW WORLD
This dish is ideal to showcase the Australian Shiraz-Grange, and other Penfolds blends, Henschke, Mt. Langi Ghiran, Hardy's Eileen, Aberfeldy, Jasper Hill, Jim Barry Armagh, Yalumba Octavius, Elderton, Giaconda, Rosemount Balmoral, Tyrells Vat 9, and Leasingham Classic are our choices.

ALTERNATIVES
Cabernet Sauvignon and blends from Yarden (Israel), Kefraya or Ksara (Lebanon), and Pago del Vicario (Spain). For something unusual, try rosé wines from Mornag (Tunisia) and Meknes (Morocco), or a red wine from Chatemp (Thailand).

India

RAAN
Roasted Leg of Lamb

Raan means "leg." This roast is a specialty of the mountainous Kashmir region of India. The subtly spiced cuisine is a legacy of Mogul rulers, who favored rich and creamy dishes.

1 leg of lamb, approx 6 lbs (3 kg)

Marinade
Zest from 1 lemon
5 tbsp lemon juice
2-inch (5-cm) piece of ginger
10 cloves garlic
1 tsp cumin powder
1 tbsp cardamoms
10 cloves
1 tsp turmeric powder
$\frac{1}{2}$ tsp chili powder
1 tbsp salt

1 cup fresh almonds
4 tbsp sugar
$1\frac{1}{4}$ cup (300 ml) yogurt
1 lemon, in wedges
Sprigs of mint
String or cord to truss the lamb

Zest one lemon and squeeze out 5 tablespoons of lemon juice. Trim the fat from the lamb. Place the leg in a deep roasting pan and prick the meat all over with a large-pronged fork down to the bone to break up the meat fibers. This will tenderize the meat, a process that ensures the success of this dish.

Blend the ingredients for the marinade into a paste. Rub it all over the lamb and prick the meat again so that the spices soak in. Tie the leg with string so that the meat stays on the bone while it is cooking. Set aside for 1 hour.

Blend the almonds, sugar, and yogurt into a purée. Spread the purée over the lamb and set aside for a further 4 hours.

Roast the lamb, uncovered, in a hot oven (430°F/220°C) for 30 minutes. Then cover the roast with aluminum foil, reduce the oven temperature to (340°F/170°C), and continue roasting for about 4 hours, basting with the meat juices occasionally.

When the lamb is cooked, transfer to a serving dish, collect the juices, and boil until the liquid has reduced by half. Pour the sauce over the lamb and serve with lemon wedges and sprigs of mint.

Full-bodied reds with good acidity from Category 6. The acidity clears the palate and enhances the rich flavors of the seasonings. Full-bodied reds are also often quite complex, with a mix of flavors that flows alongside those of the dish.

OLD WORLD
We recommend a Primitivo from Italy's Manduria area. Feudi di San Marzano and Pervini are reliable producers. Because the taste of the seasonings becomes subtle after roasting, traditional matches for roast lamb can be used.

Fine old Bordeaux (from Châteaux Cheval Blanc, Margaux, and Vieux Château Certan to the more affordable de Sainte Gemme and Canon de Brem), a stately, well-aged Rioja of traditional or modern style (Muga, Marques de Caceres, Marques de Murrieta, Marques de Arienzo, La Rioja Alta, Artadi "Grandes Anadas," Valdemar, Palacio, Roda, Marqués de Vargas, and Telmo Rodríguez) all have a place here.

NEW WORLD
Look for wines made from Zinfandel that have a few years of bottle aging. Our favorite producers are Turley, Ridge, and Rafanelli (California). Less expensive alternatives are Zinfandels from such producers as St. Amant, Westwind, and Klinka Brick.

ALTERNATIVES
Cabernet Francs from New Zealand, France's Loire Valley, and northern Italy also work well. Try Gewürztraminer. The flavors of the dish will take the lead, and the wine will be, at most, a palate-cleanser.

Indonesia

UDANG PANTUNG KUNING
Lobsters in Yellow Sauce

A real gourmet treat from Bali, this dish can also be made with crayfish or large shrimp. In Bali, coconut chunks are roasted directly on charcoal, then the charred skin is scraped off and the flesh grated to make the coconut milk. This brings a smoky flavor to the dish. You can achieve the same effect by adding liquid smoke flavoring to the coconut milk.

4 small lobsters, about 1 lb (500 g) each

Spice paste
5 red chilies
3 cloves garlic
7 shallots
2-inch (5-cm) piece of turmeric
2-inch (5-cm) piece of ginger
4 candlenuts (buah keras) or 8 macadamia nuts
1 1/2 tsp ground coriander
1/2 tsp shrimp paste (belacan), toasted
1 tomato

2 tbsp oil
2 tbsp tamarind pulp
3 stalk lemongrass, bruised
5 cups water
2 Kaffir lime leaves (limau purut)
White vinegar
4 cups coconut milk
Fried shallots to garnish

Blend all the spice ingredients together to make a paste. Heat the 2 tablespoons of oil, add the spice paste and the tamarind pulp and stir till it is well combined. Add one stalk of lemongrass and cook over moderate heat for about 5 minutes. Set aside the resulting paste.

Bring the 5 cups of water to a boil. Put the whole lobsters into the pot and simmer for 15 minutes. Do not discard the water but remove the lobsters and plunge them in iced water for 1 minute, and then drain and cut the lobsters to remove the meat.

Add the spice paste, the remaining two stalks of lemongrass, the Kaffir lime leaves, and the vinegar to the water in which the lobsters were boiled. Bring to a rapid boil and cook until the stock has reduced to 2 cups. Add the coconut milk to the stock and simmer for 10 minutes. Strain the stock into a pan, add the lobster meat, and simmer for 1 minute. Serve.

Smoke and coconut milk blend to provide the flavor base for this dish. Both these elements work well with mature reds that usually have nuances of earth, mushroom, or leather. These flavors mingle well with this complex dish.

OLD WORLD
Châteauneuf du Pape reds with a little age can be delicate in texture, yet can make the match with the flavors of this dish. Château La Nerthe, Roger Sabon, Domaine Paul Autard, Domaine de la Janasse, and St. Benoit are reliable producers. From Italy, try a Brunello di Montalcino with a few years' bottle age.

NEW WORLD
From the New World, the varieties to look for are Shiraz, Malbec, and Zinfandel, also with some bottle age.

ALTERNATIVES
Go white! White Burgundies to serve here include Michel Colin Deléger Chassagne Montrachet and Vincent Girardin's Rully or St. Aubin. Also any of the many excellent well-integrated oaked New World Chardonnays are a fine match. We like Edna Valley, Chalk Hill, and Landmark from California and Lenton Brae, Grosset, Pierro, and Rosemount from Australia. Also try Gibbston, Gravitas, Stonecroft, Te Mata, and Te Whau from New Zealand.

Vietnam

GA XOI MO
Five-Spice Hens

This dish has become popular in Vietnamese restaurants in North America. This version is deep-fried, but the birds may also be roasted. Five-spice powder contains equal parts ground cinnamon, fennel, star anise, cloves, and pepper.

2 Cornish hens or small chickens
  (about 1 $^1/_2$ lbs or 750 g each)
$^1/_2$ tsp salt
$^1/_4$ tsp five-spice powder
$^1/_3$ cup tamarind pulp
$^1/_4$ cup sugar
3 tbsp fish sauce (nam pla)
1 small red chili, seeds removed and minced
3 cloves garlic, minced
Oil for frying

Make the marinade by combining the five-spice powder and salt. Rub the hens thoroughly with the marinade and set aside for 1 hour.

Put the tamarind pulp in a bowl of boiling water and leave to stand for 5 minutes. Mash the pulp with a fork and strain. Combine the tamarind water in a small saucepan with the sugar and fish sauce. Bring the mixture to a boil over high heat and stir in the chili and garlic before turning off the heat.

Heat about 3 cups of oil in a wok or pot that will contain the hens. When the oil is bubbling, lower the hens in carefully and fry, turning over once only, till the skin is deep brown and crisp (about 20 minutes). Remove and drain and then cut into serving pieces.

Pour over the tamarind-chili sauce and serve.

Wines with a spicy, earthy tone will underscore the flavors of this dish.

OLD WORLD
Vino Nobile di Montepulciano: Poliziano, Avignonesi, and Boscarelli are among the many fine producers of this wine. Try also Rhône wines. Good producers include Sorrel, Chapoutier, and Paul Jaboulet.

NEW WORLD
Kendall-Jackson's Vintner's Reserve Zinfandel marries well with this dish. Australian and Californian Shiraz-based wines also work well, as do New World Merlots.

ALTERNATIVES
Aged sparkling wines, especially vintage Champagne. Whites like Grüner Veltliner, White Rioja, and wines made from Colombard, Greco, and Gewürtztraminer are also good partners.

Mildly Spicy & Light Smoky Flavors

The primary herbs and seasonings of the recipes in this section are candlenut, coconut, coriander seeds, fennel, parsley, saffron, mint, raw nuts (used whole or ground), and sesame oil. The sauces are yogurt or are coconut-based. This section includes creamy curries and cured meats.

We have listed specific wine suggestions for each recipe. However, you can match any of the juicy whites, medium-bodied rosés, and light red wines from Category 2 with any of the recipes in this section. The round, palate-pleasing fruitiness balanced by the crisp acidity of these wines provides a foil for the creamy, mellow flavor of the dishes. The lively, fruity, and floral fragrances of sweet aromatic wines lift the flavors of mildly spicy foods while refreshing the palate.

Thailand

TOM MAMUANG
Green Mango Salad

Unripe, green-fleshed mango salads are common throughout Southeast Asia. Recent studies have shown that this iron-rich fruit also contains powerful antioxidants. This dish is not only delicious, it is good for you!

If unripe mangos are unavailable, such green apples as Granny Smith may be substituted.

7 oz (200 g) pork
2-3 sour unripe mangos (about 1 lb, 500 g)
1 tsp salt
3 tbsp oil
3 cloves garlic, finely sliced
3 shallots, finely sliced
1 tbsp dried prawns, soaked and pounded
2 tbsp peanuts, dry-roasted and crushed
1 tbsp fish sauce (nam pla)
1 tsp dried red chili flakes

Cook the pork in boiling water. Remove and mince. Set aside.

Peel the mangoes and cut the flesh into thin slices. Rub the slices with salt and leave for 5 minutes, then rinse, drain, and set aside.

Heat 3 tablespoons of oil in a wok or deep pan and when the oil is hot, sauté the sliced garlic until it turns golden. It is important to remove the garlic quickly from the oil or it will turn brown and burn, taking on a bitter edge. Repeat with the sliced shallots. Set the garlic and shallots aside on paper towels to absorb excess oil.

Remove all but 1 tablespoon of oil from the wok. Reheat the oil and then sauté the cooked minced pork for 5 minutes. Add the prawns, peanuts, fish sauce, and the chili flakes. Mix well and turn out onto a platter to cool. Include the mango slices and the reserved garlic and shallots. Toss and serve.

The complexity of this dish calls for a wine that will not overstate its accomplishments, one made from a non-aromatic grape variety. The wine must serve as a pleasant background to the accents of the dish, rather than be a blatant flavor in its own right.

OLD WORLD
Italy has many good whites that fit the bill. Grape varieties to look for include: Greco, Insolia, and Trebbiano. The popular Pinot Grigio also works well. Among the many good producers are Jermann, Pasqua, and Russolo. From France, try Domaine Leccia's E Crose Blanc or a rosé from Domaine Pieretti (both from the island of Corsica).

NEW WORLD
Pinot Gris from New Zealand to try are Carrick and Kumeu River.

ALTERNATIVES
A Carema (a Nebbiolo-based wine from Piedmont) has attractive fresh fruitiness to underscore the interesting blend of flavors in this dish: peanuts, shrimp, and pork. Reliable producers include Ferrando, Cantina dei Produttori di Carema, and Orsolani.

Try the Pinot Blanc of Chalone Vineyards (California) or Bilancia Pinot Gris (New Zealand). Fruity rather than aromatic and grassy Sauvignon Blancs fit the bill here. We like the Geyser Peak Sauvignon Blanc from California.

China

STEAMED CHICKEN WITH HAM

The most famous ham from China comes from Xuanwei county in Yunnan province. Made in the winter, it is cured in salt or smoke-dried, resulting in a dense texture, intense flavor, and a lingering saltiness. Authentic Yunnan ham needs to be soaked overnight, cleaned, and steamed before it is ready for use. Yunnan ham is now available canned, but you may opt for any good-quality ham.

1 chicken
9 oz (300 g) mustard greens (kailan)
1 tbsp salt
1-inch (2-cm) piece of ginger, sliced
2 stalks scallions (spring onions)
3 oz (100 g) ham
1 cup (225 ml) chicken stock
1 tsp soy sauce
1 tbsp rice wine or dry sherry
1 tsp sugar
$\frac{1}{2}$ tsp sesame oil
1 tsp corn flour

Parboil the Chinese kale. Rub the salt over the chicken and stuff the cavity with the ginger and scallions. Cook the chicken in a steamer for 20 minutes.

Alternatively, fill a large pot with water and bring it to a boil. Put the chicken into the pot, cover, and turn off the heat. Cook for 30 minutes then remove the chicken. Bring the same water to a boil again, then return the partially cooked chicken to the pot, cover, and, once again, turn off the heat. Remove the chicken when it is fully cooked. This should take about 15-20 minutes. Test by inserting a fork into the thigh of the chicken; the bird is cooked when the juices run clear. Reserve the stock.

Allow the chicken to cool, discard the ginger and scallions, debone and chop the chicken into serving pieces. Slice the ham into pieces of a similar size as the chicken pieces. Arrange the chicken on a platter with a slice of ham on each piece. Fill the gaps between the meat with the cooked kale.

To make the gravy, heat 1 cup of the chicken stock, soy sauce, wine, sugar, and sesame oil over low heat. Include the corn flour and keep stirring. When the sauce has thickened, pour it over the dish and serve.

The zing of ginger, the sweet gaminess of ham, the mildness of steamed chicken – you want a wine that will accommodate all these flavors without overwhelming them. You will not go wrong with an unoaked or lightly oaked Chardonnay or Pinot Blanc from anywhere in the world.

OLD WORLD
The scents of toasted hazelnuts and mineral notes on the palate make Fiano di Avellino a fine choice. Among the many fine producers are Mastroberardino, Feudi di San Gregorio, and Di Meo. Among our favorite Pinot Blancs are Querciabella Batar (Italy), Rolly-Gassmann (Alsace, France), and Fritz Salomon (Austria).

NEW WORLD
Try Californian Pinot Blancs from Saddleback, Au Bon Climat, Steele, Byron, Arrowood, and Murphy-Goode.

ALTERNATIVES
Red wines may be served. Try Dolcetto from a reliable producer (among them G. D. Vajra, Elio Grasso, and Ceretto) or a Cabernet Franc from Friuli, Italy. Another classic Cabernet Franc with substance and freshness is Chinon, which comes from the Loire valley, France. Top producers include Bernard Baudry and Chateau de la Grille. Young St-Emilions (often based on Cabernet Franc and Merlot), have similar qualities.

When it comes to the New World, think – you've got it – vivacious Cabernet Franc! Good producers are California's Geyser Peak, Jekel, Iron-stone, Virginia's Barboursville and Prince Michel, and practically all Washington-state producers.

You may also wish to try a Dolcetto from Californian producers, such as Per Sempre and Kent Rasmussen.

China
BRAISED PORK IN SOY SAUCE

The streaky cut of pork you want for this dish must have skin and some fat. In China, it is called three-layered meat, referring to the skin, fat, and meat. Braised in dark soy sauce, it becomes a comfort food relished by the southern Chinese. Perfect with a bowl of steaming fragrant rice.

2 lbs (900 g) streaky pork
2 tbsp lard or butter
2 cloves garlic, crushed
3 shallots, pounded
1 star anise
1 tbsp sugar
2 tbsp dark soy sauce
1 tsp salt
1 cup (225 ml) water

Marinade
1 tbsp dark soy sauce
1 tsp honey
$1/2$ tsp five spice powder

Make a marinade by combining the soy sauce, honey, and five-spice powder. Marinate the pork for about 1 hour.

Heat the lard in a wok or saucepan and fry the garlic, shallots, star anise, and the sugar till the shallots turn brown. To this, add the pork and brown it on all sides.

Add 2 tablespoons dark soy sauce, salt, and half the water (about 110 ml). Cover and cook for 10 minutes. Remove the lid and continue to cook, stirring until the sauce is thick. Add the rest of the water and simmer, stirring to prevent sticking.

Cover and continue cooking at a simmer until the meat is tender (about 1 hour). Add a little more water if the sauce dries out before the meat is ready. Cool. Cut the pork into thick slices and serve.

When fatty pork enters the equation, it is always a good idea to choose a wine with good, crisp acidity that cuts through the fat. However, the wine's fruitiness should also be bold enough to complement the dish's rich flavor.

OLD WORLD
The Vigneto Enrico Cialdini Lambrusco from Chiarli has an exuberant grapey fragrance and supple strawberry and raspberry flavors, as well as zippy acidity.

NEW WORLD
Any sparkling red from Australia also has the right combination of freshness and medium body. Good producers are Seppelts (Sparkling Burgundy), Rockford (Black Shiraz), Charles Melton, Alkoomi, E & E, Brown Brothers, Leasingham, and Mitchells.

ALTERNATIVES
For a fuller, more rounded accompaniment, try Villa Bucci's Tenuta Pongelli Rosso Piceno, with its fresh, juicy amalgam of blackberry and blueberry fruit infused with a delicate mineral note. Top-end Bordeaux and Cabernet Sauvignons work as well. For something lighter, try Pinot Noirs from California by Acacia, Pedroncelli, Sebastiani, and Rutz Cellars. Pinot Noirs from Oregon such as Argyle and Brick House are also good alternatives.

India

MEEN VARUVAL
Southern Indian Fried Fish

"Varuval" indicates a fried dish, and "meen" is fish. This fried fish dish hails from the Kerala coast, where it is traditionally prepared using seer fish. Mackerel or kingfish would be just as good.

1 lb 10 oz (800 g) fish fillets or cutlets
1 1/2 cups (350 ml) oil for frying
20 curry leaves (optional)

Marinade
1/8 cup (40 ml) lemon juice
1 tsp ginger, finely chopped
1 tsp garlic, finely chopped
3 tsp turmeric
1 tsp salt

Flour mixture
4 1/2 oz (150 g) rice flour
1 1/2 oz (40 g) besan flour (gram flour)
2 tbsp chili powder
1 tsp salt

Marinade the fish in the lemon, ginger, garlic, turmeric, and salt for 30 minutes. Mix the rice and besan flours and to the mixture add the chili powder and salt.

If you are using curry leaves, strip the leaves from the stem and fry the leaves in hot oil till they are almost crisp. Reserve for garnishing.

Heat the oil in a pan or griddle. Dust the fish in the flour mixture, and shallow fry one side at a time. When both sides are done, remove, set on a plate, and garnish with the curry leaves if you are using them.

The virtues of the wines listed in Category 2 is that they offer satisfying structure, refreshing acidity, and the capacity to bring out the best in many dishes. These wines are team players! With this dish, the wine's tanginess cuts through the batter to reveal the taste of the fish itself.

OLD WORLD
In Sicily there are many good wines made from a blend of Chardonnay and Insolia grapes. A favorite of ours is Fazio's Torre dei Venti. It has a luscious scent of ripe, white-fleshed peaches and greengage plums that is echoed on a palate dancing with sprightly acidity. Another fine Chardonnay-Insolia (aka Ansonica) blend is the Chiarandà from Donnafugata. Other good European matches include Alsace Pinot Blanc and Austrian Grüner Veltliner.

NEW WORLD
Unusual Chardonnays from the U.S. to try with this dish include Pend d'Oreille (Idaho), Chateau Chantal (Michigan), and Breaux Vineyards (Virginia).

ALTERNATIVES
Try an Australian "Cab-Mac" Beaujolais style or, better, a well-chilled Beaujolais. Favorite producers are Dominique Chermette, Henri et Bernard Girin, des Nugues, Marcel Lapierre (Vin de Table), and Domaine du Vissoux. From Italy, most Dolcettos fit the bill. Some favorites are Punset, Ceretto, Settimo Aurelio, and Fontanafredda.

China

BRAISED BEAN CURD AND PORK

Bean curd, or tofu, is made by coagulating soy milk extracted from the bean. The curd has a range of textures, from silken to firm and spongy, depending on how it is processed. Bean curd is rather bland but takes on the flavors of the other ingredients in a dish. You may omit the pork to make a vegetarian dish.

3 blocks firm bean curd (4 x 2 in, 10 x 15 cm), cut into 1-inch
   (2.5-cm) cubes
$^1/_2$ lb (250 g) lean pork, boiled
2 scallions (spring onions), cut into 1.2-inch (2-cm) lengths
10 slices of canned bamboo shoots
1 small carrot, sliced
$^1/_2$ cup snow peas
$^1/_2$ cup canned baby corn
6 button mushrooms
2 tbsp soy sauce
1 tsp sugar
1 cup (225 ml) stock
1 tsp corn flour rendered in 5 tbsp cold water till smooth
4 tbsp oil

Trim off and discard the mushroom stems. Set aside. Slice the pork into thin strips.

Heat the oil in a deep pan or wok and sauté the bean curd for a minute. Remove and set aside. In the same wok, sauté the scallions, bamboo shoots, carrots, pork, snow peas, baby corn, and mushrooms for about a minute. Include the soy sauce, sugar, and the stock and then bring to a boil.

Finally, add the bean curd and simmer for 10 minutes. Thicken the dish by stirring in the rendered cornstarch, then turn off the heat. Serve hot.

The slight sweetness of the vegetables and sauce call for a wine with a broad, fruity perfume.

OLD WORLD
A well-made Soave. We particularly like the light peach and wildflower notes of a refreshing Bertani Soave, which form a perfect backdrop for the complex flavors and textures of this dish. Try also mild whites from France, such as the Chardonnay-based wines of Montagny or Viré-Clissé (the new appellation in Mâcon, Burgundy). Similarly, the wines of southwest France have a place here. Producers we like are Domaine Cauhape for dry or sweet Jurançons and Les Vignerons du Pays Basque for Irouléguy pink wines. The Vins de Pays from around France to try include Pannier Chardonnay (Jardin de la France), Domaine de Poumeyrade "Terra Sana" (Aquitaine et Charentes), Calvet de Calvet Chardonnay (d'Oc), and Moulin de Gassac "Guilhem Blanc" (Hérault).

NEW WORLD
From the New World try unoaked (or very lightly oaked) Chardonnay. Echeverria (Chile), Edward's Lake (Australia), Babich (New Zealand), Banrock Station (Australia), and Newton (California) are some good producers.

ALTERNATIVES
Pink wines, dry or lightly sweet, identified by any of the following words on the label: rosé, White Zinfandel, Cabernet Blanc, Blush, Rosato, and Rosado.

Malaysia / Singapore

SAYOR LODEH
Curried Vegetables

This is a Peranakan dish of Malay origin. Peranakan refers to the descendants of Chinese immigrants to Singapore, Malacca, and Penang who married local Malays. This cuisine reflects this blend of cultures and tastes.

10 oz (300 g) eggplant
4 shallots
2 garlic cloves, peeled
1 tsp shrimp paste
4 candlenuts or 8 macadamia nuts
2 tsp ground coriander
3 cups (700 ml) coconut milk
2 slices galangal (lengkuas), crushed
5 red chilies sliced into rings, seeds discarded
1 tsp salt
8 oz (250 g) green beans
4 oz (125 g) bamboo shoots
1 carrot
8 oz (250 g) cabbage, shredded

Cut the eggplant in half, lengthwise, and slice it into bite-sized pieces. Soak the cut eggplant in a little salted water to remove the bitter juices. When soft, rinse and drain. Cut the green beans into 1-inch (2.5-cm) lengths and the bamboo shoots and carrot into bite-sized pieces.

Grind the shallots, garlic, shrimp paste, and candlenuts in a food processor. Add the coriander and a teaspoon of water to the mixture and stir to make a paste.

Put the paste and the coconut milk in a pot and bring to a boil, stirring occasionally to prevent burning. Add the galangal, chili, and salt. Reduce the heat and add the beans, carrot, and bamboo shoots. When almost cooked, add the eggplant and cabbage. Continue cooking over a low fire till the cabbage and eggplant are just tender. Serve.

A well-structured dry rosé will lift the flavor of this dish and refresh the palate.

OLD WORLD
Montepulciano D'Abruzzo Cerasuolo from a reliable producer like Masciarelli, Nicodemi, or Illuminati fits the bill, as does the Puglian rosé Salice Salentino Rosato (reliable producers include Conte Zecca, Cosimo Taurino, and Vallone). Also a Bardolino or a young Dolcetto will work well. Other good dry rosés can be found in the French region of Provence. Top producers in the Côtes de Provence include Domaine d'Ott and Mas Ste. Berthe.

NEW WORLD
Many New World rosés have a healthy dose of residual sugar, so be sure to look for a truly dry wine.

ALTERNATIVE
An aromatic white, such as a Riesling, will add a decisive dimension to the flavor. It is not a choice for everyone, but certainly worth experimenting with.

Indonesia

OPOR AYAM
Mild Chicken Curry

Indonesia's historic spice trade drew merchants and colonists from India, China, Africa, the Americas, the Netherlands, Portugal, and Britain. Each group brought its own ingredients and cooking techniques. The melding of these disparate cultures led to the creation of delicious and popular dishes with a distinctively Indonesian flavor. Coconut in its many forms (oil, milk, and flesh) is a frequent ingredient, as are pastes made from blending spices with coconut milk.

4 chicken breasts with skin on, each cut into 4 parts
3 cloves garlic, crushed
I tsp salt
$^1/_2$ tsp black pepper
2 tsp grated ginger
3 candlenuts or 6 macadamia nuts, crushed
3 tsp ground coriander
I tsp ground cumin
$^1/_4$ tsp ground galangal (lengkuas)
4 tbsp oil
2 medium onions, sliced
3 cups (700 ml) coconut milk
6 curry leaves
I stalk lemongrass, root end and leaves removed, bruised
2-inch (5-cm) stick of cinnamon
I tsp lemon juice

Combine the garlic, salt, pepper, ginger, candlenuts, coriander, cumin, and the galangal in a bowl with 1 tablespoon of oil. Rub this marinade all over and inside the chicken. Set aside for 1 hour.

Heat 2 tablespoons of oil and fry the onions until they turn golden, then remove. Add 1 tablespoon of oil and fry the chicken pieces until they begin to color. Add 1 cup of coconut milk, the curry leaves, the lemongrass stem, and the cinnamon stick. Cook uncovered and stir occasionally until the chicken is cooked. Add the 2 remaining cups of coconut milk, the lemon juice, and season with some salt. Heat through and serve.

Coconut has a creamy, mellow texture and flavor that will be balanced and brightened by a wine with lively acidity.

OLD WORLD
A blended white from Friuli will provide zesty, palate-cleansing acidity as well as a broad fruit flavor and an intriguing fragrance. An excellent one is the versatile Vintage Tunina from Jermann. This pale gold wine is zippy and refreshing, with a touch of cloves on the nose. On the palate it is supple, with a satiny texture and attractive precise notes of greengage plums. Terre Alte (a blended white) from Livio Felluga is also very good with this dish. Another interesting partner would be a Friulano from Friuli.

NEW WORLD & OLD WORLD
Chardonnay, of course, also works well, brightening the mellow curry taste of this dish. Try a Mâcon-Villages from France such as Bicheron, Deux Roches, Roger Luquet, Mommessin, or your own New World favorite. Both California and Australia have world-class reputations for the quality of their Chardonnays.

ALTERNATIVE
A medium-sweet sparkling wine such as Asti Spumante, Demi-Sec Cava, and demi-sec Champagne or sparkling Zinfandel.

Indonesia

SAMBAL BABI
Pork Sambal

On the Indonesian island of Bali (unlike the neighboring islands of Java and Sumatra, which are predominantly Muslim) pork, or *babi*, is eaten and, indeed, roasted suckling pig (Babi Guling) is a specialty.

1½ lbs (700 g) pork belly, cut into 1½-inch (4-cm) cubes
1½ cups (350 ml) coconut milk
1 stalk lemongrass, root end and leaves removed, bruised
2 tsp grated ginger
2 small onions, chopped
4 cloves garlic, crushed
1 tsp chili powder
1 tsp shrimp paste (belacan)
1 tsp ground coriander
1 tsp ground cumin
2 tsp sugar
1 tsp salt

Bring half the coconut milk (about 175 ml) slowly to a boil in a pot. Add all the other ingredients as well as the pieces of pork. Stir constantly to prevent curdling.

If the gravy turns out to be too thick, add half a cup of water. Simmer until the pork is tender and almost all the liquid is absorbed (about 1 hour). Add the remaining coconut milk and continue cooking for about 10 minutes. Serve.

The texture and weight of creamy coconut milk is brightened by a wine with crisp acidity. Such a wine is also good at cleansing the palate should there be any fattiness in the pork.

OLD WORLD
A Dolcetto d'Asti from the Piedmont region of Italy has the necessary weight and freshness on the palate. There are many good producers. With their elegant tannins, Blaufränkisch from Austria and Cabernet Francs (St. Nicolas de Bourgueil, Saumur Champigny) from the Loire valley also share this flavor profile.

NEW WORLD
From the New World look for unoaked Cabernet Francs and Grenaches.

ALTERNATIVE
The softness on the palate of a Crémant d'Alsace or a Satèn from Franciacorta echoes the velvetiness of the dish.

Indonesia

RENDANG
Beef or Mutton Dry Curry

Originating from the western part of Sumatra, Padang food has come to represent Indonesian cuisine in much of the world. Padang dishes tend to be hot and spicy and are often seasoned with a mixture of spring onions, garlic, turmeric, and coconut milk. This dried beef curry (rendang) is a speciality.

1 lb (500 g) beef or mutton, cut into 1-inch (2.5-cm) cubes
10 dried chilis, seeds removed and soaked in water to soften
8 shallots
12 1/2 oz (400 g) grated coconut, toasted till lightly brown
3 cups (675 ml) coconut milk
4 tbs coriander powder
1/2 tsp cumin powder
1 stalk lemongrass, root end and leaves removed, bruised
1 tsp chopped galangal (lengkuas)
2 kaffir lime leaves (limau purut)
1 turmeric leaf (optional)
2 tsp sugar
1 tsp salt

Grind the dried chilies, shallots, and grated coconut in a food processor to make a smooth paste.

Combine this paste, the coconut milk, and all the other ingredients (except the meat) in a pot. Bring to a boil and then add the meat. Cook uncovered, simmering till the meat is tender (about 2 hours). Stir regularly to prevent sticking or burning and add half a cup of water if it becomes too dry. The finished dish should not be soupy but have a thick gravy.

If you have used the lemongrass stem, kaffir lime leaves, and turmeric leaves, remove them before serving. You can, of course, include them in your presentation, but they should not be eaten.

The texture and weight of creamy coconut milk are brightened by a wine with zippy acidity. Such a wine is also a good at cleansing the palate should there be any fattiness in the mutton.

OLD WORLD
A good Bardolino from Le Fraghe or Guerrieri Rizzardi, Corte Gardoni, and Cavalchina or any of the reliable producers in the zone. Do not choose a Bardolino Superiore with this dish as the word "*Superiore*" indicates that the wine has been given extra aging, while this dish calls for the fresh fruity flavors of a young Bardolino. Look to the Loire valley for fresh, invigorating young reds (Saumur and Bourgueil). Alsace offers Pinot Noir and in Bordeaux, there is a light red called Clairet.

NEW WORLD
Blended wines from the New World have their place here. From California, we suggest Peju Carnival, St. Supery Virtu, and Cool Fish "White."

ALTERNATIVES
The key to finding a New World red to match this dish is to find one that is made entirely in stainless steel vats or uses wood sparingly. Examples are Simonsig Pinotage and Van Loveren River Red (from South Africa), Rocky Gully Shiraz, Peter Lehmann Barossa Grenache, and Mitchelton Mourvèdre Light Red (from Australia). Try also a fruity and lightly sweet Moscato d'Asti (La Ghersa, La Badia, and Braida are favorites).

GOMA AE
Spinach Salad with Sesame Sauce

This is a delightful summer salad with sweet sake and sesame flavors filtering through slightly bitter spinach. It is very simple to make and can be served as a first course or as an appetizer.

12 oz (375 g) spinach

Dressing
4 tbsp sesame paste or tahini
3 tbsp white sesame seeds
2 tbsp sesame oil
$1/2$ tsp sugar
2 tsp soy sauce
2 tbsp sake (Japanese rice wine)

Heat the white sesame seeds in a small frying pan over medium heat till light golden, shaking to prevent burning. The sesame seeds will continue to brown after they are removed from the heat, so do not overcook them. Grind 2 tablespoons of these sesame seeds using a mortar and pestle. Set aside. Reserve the remaining tablespoon for garnishing.

Prepare the dressing by mixing the sesame paste with the sesame oil, sugar, soy sauce, sake, and ground sesame seeds. If it is too thick, add a little water. The consistency should be that of a smooth, thin paste.

Parboil the spinach for about 30 seconds till just cooked and quickly transfer it to a bath of cold water to stop the cooking process. This will ensure that the spinach remains bright green. Drain and chop the spinach into 1-inch (2.5-cm) lengths and stir in the dressing. Arrange on a flat serving plate and sprinkle on the reserved sesame seeds. Chill before serving.

Sesame and soy dominate the taste of this dish. Light white wines and fruity red wines with soft tannins will not clash with the salad's dressing.

OLD WORLD
A creamy sparkling Satèn from Italy's Franciacorta DOCG (*Denominazione di origine controllata e garantita*) zone would be ideal. Pinot Grigio also has the versatility and fruitiness to underscore the lightly nutty flavors of sesame and soy. If you prefer a red wine, try a well-chilled Teroldego from the Trentino region of Italy. Top producers include Fratelli Dorigati and Foradori. From France, choose any good Côtes du Rhônes; from Guigal, Delas Frères, Chapoutier, and Jaboulet to Domaine de la Maurelle, Beaucastel, and Les Aphillanthes.

NEW WORLD
White varieties include Pinot Blanc, Colombard, and Johannisberg Riesling. For reds, try the varietals of Pinot Noir, Grenache, and any lightly oaked Cabernet Franc.

ALTERNATIVES
Woody whites and soft-tannin red wines from Category 3 can be ventured.

Spicy & Smoky Flavors

The hallmarks of the recipes in this section are the tingle of spices and the mellow sensation of smoke. The primary herbs and flavorings are mild chilies, cumin, mace, tamarind, saffron, and sesame seeds. The primary sauces and pastes include: peanut-based sauces, oyster sauce, mild chili sauce, and curry paste, sesame paste, and tamarind paste.

You can match any of the wines in Category 3 with any of the recipes in this section. The flavor of the woody whites echoes the mellowness of the spices and the nut sauces, while the fruity, soft-tannin reds merge with the juicy richness of meats and meaty fish. Many people find that the rich tones of Category 7 wines add an interesting dimension to dishes with nutty flavors.

Thailand

KAENG PHET PET YANG
Duck and Lychees in Red Curry

The most common Thai curry is red curry. Red curry paste is a blend of dry red chili, shallot, garlic, galangal, lemongrass, cilantro root, peppercorn, coriander, salt, shrimp paste, and the zest of kaffir lime. It is different from green curry paste, which uses fresh green chili. Both are available in bottles from Asian stores.

Red curry paste
$1/2$ tbsp ground coriander
$1/2$ tsp ground cumin
$1/2$ tsp shrimp paste (belacan)
5 dried red chilies
2 shallots
6 cloves garlic
1-inch (2.5-cm) piece of galangal (lengkuas)
1 stalk lemongrass
1 tsp minced kaffir lime (limau purut)
1 stalk cilantro leaves (coriander0
10 peppercorns

Take the white stem of the lemongrass and discard the leaves. Trim off the root end and slice the white stem into rounds. Soak the dried red chilies in hot water for 10 minutes and discard the seeds. Blend all the ingredients together in a food processor. Add water a little at a time and grind till a smooth paste is obtained. This red curry paste can be frozen and used as required.

$12 1/2$ oz (400 g) roasted duck breast, cut in bite-sized pieces
2 cups (450 ml) coconut milk
$1/3$ cup red curry paste
4 cherry tomatoes
10 oz (300 g) canned lychee, drained
2 tbsp fish sauce
$1/4$ tsp salt
$1 1/2$ tsp sugar
5 kaffir lime leaves (limau purut), shredded
1 red chili, sliced and deseeded
$1/2$ cup (125 g) sweet Thai basil leaves (horapha)

Heat half of the coconut milk (1 cup) over low heat. When it starts to thicken, add the red curry paste and stir constantly to prevent the mixture from sticking to the pan.

As the oil separates, include the duck meat and mix well. Add the remaining coconut milk, fish sauce, salt, and sugar, and simmer for 5 minutes. Add the cherry tomatos, lychees, kaffir lime leaves, and red chili and bring to a boil again. Put in the sweet basil leaves just before serving, submerging them to prevent them from discoloring.

The richness of this duck dish calls for a fruity wine with good acidity that is capable of refreshing the palate. Toasty oak-aged wines make the liaison with the coconut milk.

OLD WORLD
Rosso di Montepulciano has juicy Sangiovese cherry fruit and is easy to drink. Among reliable producers are Poliziano, Vecchia Cantina Redi, La Calonica and Fattoria del Cerro. Also try a moderately aged (at least three years) St. Emilion, Canon, or Canon Fronsac (Bordeaux), whose tannins have softened. Favorite producers are Canon-Moueix, Fontenil, La Croix Canon, and Mazeris.

NEW WORLD
Many California producers also make excellent Sangiovese wines. Among them are Altamura, Rutherford Hill, Shafer, Staglin, Silverado, and Chappellet.

ALTERNATIVES
Pinot Noirs can also be served here, such as those of Freeman, Tandem, Summerland Chamisal, Kendall-Jackson, MacMurray Ranch, Clos du Bois, Muirwood, Sterling, La Crema, Frei and Cambrai (California), Carabella, Panther Creek, Medici, Domaine Drouhin, and Ponzi (Oregon), Bass Philip and Coldstream Hills (Australia), and Waipara West, Tohu, Felton Road, Matua Valley, Mount Difficulty, and Morton (New Zealand).

Mellow Chilean Cabernet Sauvignons from Caliterra, Casablanca, Montes, and Valdivieso are also good. Try also top-end Chardonnays such as Pierro (Australia), Kumeu River (New Zealand), Chalk Hill (California), and any Bâtard-Montrachet (France).

Thailand

KAYANG
Grilled Chicken

This popular Thai snack comes in many versions, which vary from region to region, but the best place to sample this traditional tidbit is at the country's major train stations!

1 $\frac{1}{2}$ lbs (700 g) chicken parts
1 tsp ground pepper
3 leaf cilantro (coriander leaves)
4 cloves garlic
3 tbsp lime juice
$\frac{1}{2}$ tbsp fish sauce
$\frac{1}{2}$ tbsp light soy sauce
$\frac{1}{4}$ tsp sugar

Blend together the pepper, cilantro, garlic, lime juice, fish sauce, light soy sauce, and sugar in a food processor. Marinate the chicken with this mixture and refrigerate for at least 2 hours.

Heat a grill and, when hot, grill the chicken until its juices run clear and the skin is crisp. Serve with bottled Thai sweet chili sauce or your favorite chili condiment.

The spicy, smoky flavor of an oaky white echoes the flavor of the grilled chicken.

OLD WORLD
A favorite is Avignonesi's Il Marzocco (85% Chardonnay, 15% Sauvignon Blanc). It has a lively lemon note that lifts the round creamy fruit, with warm spices coming through on the finish. Other good woody whites include Condrieus from Chapoutier, Paul Jaboulet, and Guigal.

NEW WORLD
Almost any oaked Chardonnay or Viognier from California or Australia makes an attractive alternative match. We particularly like Grgich Hills, Bonterra, Eberle, Zaca Mesa, McDowell, Pride Mountain (California), and Geoff Weaver (Australia).

ALTERNATIVES
Wyndham Estate Bin 555 Shiraz, with its generous and spicy plum and strawberry fruit is the red wine choice here. It adds another dimension of flavor. Also try such Syrahs-Rhone blends from Washington state as Canon de Sol, Seven Hills, Gamache Vintners, Fidelitas, and McCrea as well as Côtes du Rhône red wines. Perrin & Fils Vinsobres is a particular favorite.

China

IMPERIAL-STYLE GRILLED SPARERIBS

It has been said that imperial-style food has existed in China ever since there were emperors and palaces. Some dishes, of course, included rare delicacies, but there were also foods that were just improvements on those enjoyed by commoners, using everyday ingredients. Grilled or barbecued spareribs, like sweet-and-sour pork, may well have been concocted by Chinese chefs in America to whet Western appetites. Still, these dishes are found on the menus of well-respected Chinese restaurants today.

2 lbs (1 kg) pork spareribs
2 tbsp lard or butter
1 chili, seeds removed and chopped

Marinade
2 tbsp tomato sauce
2 tbsp Hoisin sauce
1 tbsp honey
1 tbsp sweet chili sauce
1 tbsp sherry
2 tbsp light soy sauce
$^1/_2$ tbsp lime juice
1 tsp five-spice powder
1 tsp chopped garlic
1 tsp pepper

Wash and towel dry the spareribs. Combine the ingredients for the marinade and marinate the pork for about 4 hours in the refrigerator.

Line a baking tray with foil to collect the juices and drippings for basting. Heat a grill or oven to 450°F (230°C). Brush the meat with the lard and grill or bake for 10 minutes, turning once to brown the other side. Reduce the heat to 300°F (150°C) and cook for a further 20 minutes, basting the meat with the drippings and marinade. Garnish with the chopped chili. This dish can be served hot or cold.

A fruity, low-tannin red blends with the rich sweetness of the marinade and of the meat.

OLD WORLD
Sangiovese di Romagna Ceregio from Fattoria Zerbina has a fresh yet mellow black-cherry fragrance that compliments this smoky dish. Similar qualities are found in the easy-drinking styles of Nero D'Avola-based wines from Sicily. Top producers include Duca di Salaparuta, Settesoli, Zonin, and Fazio.

Valpolicella also works well. Good producers are Begali, Corte Sant'Alda, Pasqua, and Villa Monteleone. Try red Burgundies from Bouchard, Anne Gros, Hubert Lignier, Joseph Roty, Jean Grivot, Domaine Dujac, Henri Gouges, Robert Arnoux, and the domains of Faiveley or Drouhin.

NEW WORLD
Try Banrock Station Shiraz-Cabernet, Bear Crossing Cabernet-Merlot, or Rosemount Grenache-Shiraz, (Australia); Bogle Petit Sirah, Rabbit Ridge Zinfandel, Kendall-Jackson Syrah or Sutter Home Pinot Noir (California); Concha y Toro Merlot (Chile); and Michel Torino Malbec or the Masi Tupungato Passo Doble (Argentina). All are reasonably priced.

ALTERNATIVES
A Riesling Spätlese's sweetness bonds with the honey and savory flavors of the dish. Also try a spicy Pinot Gris from Alsace, an Italian Pinot Grigio with a mineral note, or a clean, crisp green-appley New Zealand Pinot Grigio. All display a mellow roundedness of flavor that is ideal with these succulent spareribs. Other good Pinot Gris to try include Maysara, Civello, and Lange from Oregon. The adventurous may also try a dry sherry.

Japan

BEEF RAMEN
Beef Noodle Soup

It has been said that ramen is not just a noodle soup but an institution. Ramen in Japan is a fast food, served from "counter" restaurants, where millions of people literally slurp up the noodles each day. Apparently, like aerating wine while drinking, the intake of air while slurping brings out the flavor of the soup. Ramen originated in China, and a number of toppings, like roasted pork and beef, hark back to its roots.

1³/₄ lbs (800 g) beef short ribs
8 oz (250 g) fresh ramen noodles
¹/₃ cup (80 g) white miso paste
¹/₃ cup (80 g) light soy sauce
¹/₄ cup (60 ml) mirin
1 egg, hard-boiled
1 stalk scallion (spring onion), sliced

Marinade
1 cup (225 ml) mirin
¹/₂ cup medium-sweet sherry
1 cup (225 ml) soy sauce
1-inch (2.5-cm) piece of ginger, sliced

Cut the short ribs crosswise into ¹/₂-inch (1-cm) slices, keeping the bone attached.

To make the marinade, first remove the alcohol content from the mirin by bringing it to a boil in a small saucepan. Turn off the heat and add all the other ingredients of the marinade. Allow to cool and marinate the ribs overnight in the refrigerator.

The following day, make the ramen broth by bringing 5 cups of water in a large pot to a boil. Turn down the heat to a simmer and stir in the miso paste, soy sauce, and mirin. Heat the soup through, but do not let it boil.

Meanwhile, remove the meat from the refrigerator and wipe off the excess marinade. Grill the ribs under a hot broiler or over a charcoal fire, turning once. It should take 5 minutes for the beef to cook.

Place the fresh noodles in individual serving bowls, pour on the broth, place the grilled beef short ribs on top, and garnish with the sliced scallions and half a hard-boiled egg. Serve.

This dish has a soft, broad aroma that remains intact when you serve a floral scented wine.

OLD WORLD
We suggest a Verdicchio Superiore from a top producer like Villa Bucci or Garofoli. A Château Grillet is rare. Easier to find French Viogniers are made by Delas Freres, Dumazet, Alain Paret, and Georges Vernay in Condrieu. The other white wines of the Rhone, such as Hermitage Blanc, St. Joseph Blanc (made from Marsanne and Roussanne grapes) hold their own here too.

NEW WORLD
New World Viogniers work well here, but they have to be fruity. We like the tropical fruit flavor of the Viognier from Pacific Star and the pear-fruited Viognier of Alban Vineyards, both from California. You could also try the Viognier of Elemental Cellars (Oregon).

ALTERNATIVES
A well-made Friulano, with its medium body and almost creamy fragrance, works well with this dish. Also try soft and supple reds such as the Merlots of Leonetti (Washington state), Whitehall Lane, and Beringer (California). For something lighter, try the Patton Valley Pinot Noir rosé (Oregon).

India

TANDOORI CHICKEN

The tandoor is the traditional coal-fired Indian clay oven. Its intense heat cooks meat very quickly and makes food crispy on the outside while retaining juiciness inside. This is the secret of the taste of authentic tandoori dishes.

10 chicken parts, skinned
$^1/_3$ cup ghee
3 lettuce leaves
1 lemon, wedged
1 small onion, sliced

Marinade
1 onion
5 cloves garlic
2-inch (5-cm) piece of ginger
$^1/_2$ tsp sugar
1 tsp salt
$^1/_2$ cup (115 ml) yogurt
1 tsp chili powder
2 tbsp tomato puree
Pinch of saffron
2 tbsp lemon juice
1 tsp cumin powder
1 tsp garam masala
$^1/_2$ cup (115 ml) cream

Blend all the marinade ingredients together in a food processor to obtain a paste. Make deep cuts in the chicken with a sharp knife and rub the meat thoroughly with the marinade. Leave to stand for 3 hours.

Heat an oven to about 350 °F (180°C) and roast the marinated chicken for 20 minutes while constantly basting it with the ghee.

Serve on a bed of lettuce with wedges of lemon and sliced onion.

Note: Chicken may be substituted with shrimp or fish without altering the taste of the dish much. Use twenty shelled shrimp or firm-fleshed fish fillets cut into chunks. Roasting times are 10 minutes for the shrimp and 8 minutes for the fish.

Fresh, juicy fruit fragrances in wine cut through the smokiness and enhance the aromas and flavors of the tandoori.

OLD WORLD
A Nebbiolo from the Valtellina zone of Italy has the necessary suppleness and full fruitiness for tandoori. Among top producers are Nino Negri and Triacca. Tempranillo, with its strawberry or cherry fruit flavors and sweet finish, also works well. Reliable pro-ducers from Spain include Guelbenzu, Chivite, El Coto, Muga, Marques de Caceres, Artadi, and Valduero.

NEW WORLD
Try a Pinot Noir from New Zealand such as Cloudy Bay, Grove Mill, Georges Michel, Herzog, Thornbury, Churton (all in the Marlborough region), and the Te Kairanga, Martin-borough Vineyards, Ata Rangi, Escarp-ment, and Schubert (Martinborough county). Among excellent California producers of Nebbiolo are Byington and Bonny Doon.

ALTERNATIVES
Well-made, medium-priced Montepulciano d'Abruzzos are very versatile food wines. Top producers include Gianni Masciarelli, Dino Illuminati, Bruno Nicodemi, and Luigi Cataldi Madonna. Or try Beaujolais Crus from producers such as Duboeuf, Chignard, G Vincent, Domaine de Garanches, Buis, G Viornery, Charvet, Meziat, and Brouillard. Each producer makes a range of styles from lightly scented Chiroubles, Régnié, and Brouilly crus to the fruity wines of Fleurie and St. Amour to the Morgon and Chénas crus.

Unoaked or lightly oaked Merlots and Barberas from California or Chile share the same qualities. The adven-turous may wish to try chilled dry sherry.

Indonesia

SATAY

Different styles of satay and its accompanying dipping sauces are found in Indonesia, Malaysia, and Singapore. Indonesian sate (as the word is spelled there) is more gently grilled than Malay satay, which is deliciously chewy and charred over very hot coals. The satay of the Chinese Hainanese immigrants to the region features fatty pork and a sauce served with a dollop of finely grated pineapple.

Peanut Sauce

4 tbsp oil	1 tbsp dried tamarind
1 stalk lemongrass	1 cup (225 ml) hot water
2 tsp shrimp paste [belachan]	1 tsp chili powder
1 medium onion, chopped	2 tbsp sugar
3 cloves garlic, minced	1 tsp dark soy sauce
6 oz (190 g) roasted peanuts	1 cup (225 ml) coconut milk

Trim off and discard the root end and leaves of the lemongrass. Slice the white stem into rounds. Put the shrimp paste on a spoon and toast it over a fire until it is fragrant.

Blend 2 tablespoons of oil, the lemongrass, onion, garlic, and the toasted shrimp paste in a food processor to obtain a spice paste. Remove and reserve. Crush the peanuts to the texture of coarse sand in the food processor. Set aside. Soak the tamarind in the hot water, mash it with the back of a spoon till the pulp disintegrates, and strain. Keep the liquid.

Heat the remaining 2 tablespoons of oil and sauté the spice paste until it is fragrant. Then add the crushed peanuts, tamarind liquid, chili powder, sugar, and dark soy sauce. At this stage, a cup (225 ml) of coconut milk can be added if you prefer a creamier sauce. Simmer, stirring till the sauce thickens.

1 1/2 lbs (700 g) meat (chicken fillets, round steak, or lamb steaks)

2 tsp ground turmeric	1 tbsp sugar
2 tsp ground cumin	4 tbsp thick coconut milk
2 tsp ground fennel	3 onions, wedged
2 tbsp finely grated lemon zest	1 cucumber, wedged
1 tsp salt	Thin bamboo skewers

Soak the skewers in water for 3 hours so that they do not burn over the fire. Cut the meat into 3/4-inch (2-cm) cubes, leaving some of the fat. Combine all the other ingredients in a bowl and marinate the meat for 2 hours, then thread four pieces of the meat onto each skewer. Grill the meat over hot coals or under a broiler until the meat is cooked. Serve with the sauce, onions, and cucumber wedges.

The woody element in a barrique-aged white echoes the flavors of the smoke-infused meat and peanuts used in the sauce.

OLD WORLD
A good Trebbiano d'Abruzzo, such as Gianni Masciarelli's Marina Cvetic Trebbiano, with its citrusy freshness combined with mellow oak, creates an ideal match for sate (and other dishes that feature a peanut sauce).

NEW WORLD
Lightly wooded wines made from Chardonnay or Viognier also make excellent matches, whether they come from France or the New World.

ALTERNATIVES
Sweet rich wines, ranging from Muscat de Beaumes-de-Venise to even port; serve them well chilled. Other sweet wines include those of Feiler Artinger Ausbruchs (Austria), D'Arenberg, de Bortoli and Yalumba (Australia), Santa Rita and Undurraga (Chile), Wente and Dolce (California), Maculan Torcolato (Italy), and Aureum Vinum and Istvan Szepsy (Hungary).

If you want a red, the blends of Sangiovese and Montepulciano found in the Rosso Piceno zone of Italy's Marche region work very well. The Montepulciano grape variety has the soft fruitiness to blend well with the meat, while the Sangiovese gives the blend a silky elegance. Reliable producers include Villa Bucci, Cocci Grifoni, Terre Cortesi Moncaro, and Tenuta de Angelis. From Spain, try a young red Rioja.

Any woody white wine, especially Pinot Blanc (also known as Pinot Bianco) or Semillon-Sauvignon blends have a place here.

Indonesia

GADO GADO
Indonesian Salad with Peanut Sauce

This classic Indonesian salad, with its creamy sauce, can also be found in Singapore and Malaysia, where the sauce is gritty with coarsely ground peanuts. The texture of the sauce is, of course, determined by how fine you grind the peanuts. The vegetables in this recipe are those commonly used, but you may include any other hard or leafy greens you choose, and even carrots.

5 oz (150 g) long beans, cut into 1-inch (2.5-cm) lengths
4 oz (115 g) cauliflower, cut into florets
4 oz (115 g) bean sprouts, root ends removed
5 oz (150 g) water convolvulus (kangkong), cut into 4-inch (10-cm) lengths
$1/4$ head white cabbage, shredded
5 oz (150 g) fermented soybean cake (tempe), cut into strips and fried till crisp
2 hard-boiled eggs, quartered
2 potatoes, boiled in their skins and then peeled and wedged
$1/2$ cucumber, wedged
1 cake fried tofu, cut into 1-inch (2.5-cm) cubes
Prawn crackers (krupuk), optional

Peanut Sauce
Sauce from the satay recipe (see page 124)

Blanch the long beans, cauliflower, beansprouts, water convolvulus, and cabbage separately, each in slightly salted water till cooked. Drain.

Arrange the cooked vegetables and the remaining ingredients on a serving dish. Serve the heated satay sauce in a deep bowl on the side.

Provide serving bowls for guests to choose their own mix of salad ingredients and ladle the sauce on individual servings.

The flavor of this dish is distinguished by the nutty sauce that is used as a dressing. As for satay, a woody white is called for here. You will not go wrong with practically any Chardonnay from California, Chile, or Australia.

NEW WORLD AND OLD WORLD
We feel that a medium-oaky Chardonnay really matches the nutty flavor of the sauce. Good examples are Chardonnays from Wolf Blass and Jamiesons Run (Australia), San Pedro, Gato Blanco (Chile), and Gallo Turning Leaf (California). Antinori's Chardonnay from its Tormaresca estate in Puglia also has very well integrated wood and broad fruit. Easy drinking and affordable wines such as Le Cadet "Chardonnay Pays d'Oc," Barton & Guestier (B&G) Réserve Vigne Rare "Pays d'Oc" from France and Enate (Spain) have similar qualities.

ALTERNATIVES
To match the sauce, have sweet rich wines: Muscat de Beaumes-de-Venise, wines with the term "beerenauslese," Tokaji, ice wines, botrytised wines, and port.

India

MASALA GRILLED FISH

Garam is Hindi for "warm" and masala means "spice." Garam masala is a classic spice mix consisting of black pepper, cloves, cinnamon, cardamom, cumin seeds, bay leaves, and coriander seeds, but in as many varying proportions as there are cooks in India. It forms the backbone of many Indian recipes.

1³/₄ lbs (800 g) firm fish fillets
   (salmon, tuna, swordfish, monkfish)
Juice of 2 lemons
Salt
2 oz (50 g) green chilies, chopped
2 oz (50 g) shallots, chopped
2 oz (50 g) ginger, peeled and chopped
1 tbsp garam masala
1 tsp turmeric

Season the fish fillets with the lemon juice and salt.

Blend the green chilies, shallots, ginger, garam marsala, and turmeric in a food processor to obtain a thick paste, adding a little water if necessary. Coat the fish pieces on both sides with the paste. Grill fish on both sides till done (about 3 minutes each side). Serve.

Well-structured, richly flavored wines will stand up to meaty fish with a strong spice component.

OLD WORLD
The Vin Jaune and Vin de Paille of France's Jura region have a nutty pungent flavor and make for an unusual match. A good example of the wines is Château Chalon. Try also the sweeter Macvin Jura (containing grape juice) from Domaine de la Pinte. Emilio Lustau, Valdespino, and Gonzalez Byass are good European producers of sherry whose wines would go with this dish.

NEW WORLD
From the New World, try a sherry from Seppelts called Seppeltsfield Amontillado DP96 or the Marsanne of Chateau Tahbilk (Australia).

ALTERNATIVES
If nutty *rancio* style wines are not to your taste, try dry, crisp white wines that cut through the spice and the fish flavors and cleanse the palate. Rieslings, Grüner Veltliners, dry Semillons, Colombards, and Chenin Blancs will then be the wines of choice.

Red wine alternatives include the full-bodied Pinotages of Kanonkop, Morgenhof, Warwick Estate, Stellenzicht, and last but not least, Diemersfontein – all from South Africa. The Chilean Carmenères of Carmen, Caliterra, and Luis Felipe Edwards are also good.

Singapore / Malaysia

LAKSA LEMAK

Laksa comes in many versions, defined by the style of the gravy and named for the place where it is found. Thus, you have Penang assam laksa with a sour fish stock, Johor laksa with a sour clear fish stock, and Sarawak laksa with a dark stock. The version below is the one found in Malacca and Singapore that features a rich coconut milk gravy.

2¹/₂ lb (1.2 kg) thick rice noodles
1 lb (500 g) fish cake, sliced
¹/₂ cup shelled cockles
1 lb (500 g) shrimp
1¹/₄ lb (625 g) bean sprouts, root ends removed
1 cucumber, peeled, cored, and shredded
A bunch Vietnamese mint (daun kesom), finely shredded

Spice mix
³/₄-inch (2-cm) piece of turmeric
³/₄-inch (2-cm) piece of galangal
15 dried chilies
5 red chilies
6 candlenuts [buah keras]
2 tbsp shrimp paste [belacan]

8 oz (250 g) shallots
1 tbsp ground coriander
2 oz (60 g) dried prawns
1 tbsp sugar
1 tbsp salt

Gravy
1 cup (225 ml) oil
2 stalks lemongrass, bruised
3 cups coconut milk

1 tsp salt
1 tsp sugar

Blanch the thick rice noodles in boiling water until they are cooked but not soggy. Remove, plunge in cold water, and drain in a colander. Blanch the bean sprouts in the same water, then remove and drain. Cut off and discard the leaves of the lemongrass. Trim off the root end and bruise the white stem with the flat of a cleaver. Grind the spice mix in a food processor to obtain a fine paste. Set aside.

Boil 2 cups (450 ml) of water with 1 teaspoon of salt and 1 teaspoon of sugar. Cook the shrimp in this liquid. Strain and reserve the stock. Shell and devein the shrimp and slice them in two along the spine. Set aside.

To make the gravy, first heat the oil in a large pot. Fry the prepared spice paste together with the lemongrass till the oil rises and the spices are fragrant. Add the reserved shrimp stock and the coconut milk. Bring this gravy to a boil, stirring constantly to prevent it from curdling, then leave to simmer over low heat for 5 minutes.

Place the bean sprouts and vermicelli in individual serving bowls, adding the shrimp, fish cake, and cockles. Pour over the simmering sauce, and garnish with cucumber and Vietnamese mint.

White wines that offer sensations of butter, vanilla, and toast are the order of the day here because they mirror the texture and flavor of the coconut milk.

NEW WORLD
New World Chardonnays work especially well here, given their rich ripe fruit and often heavier dose of oak to balance the fruit and residual sweetness in the wine. Some favorites are Gibbston Valley (NZ) and Lake's Folly Chardonnay (Australia). Other good wines to try are Catena Zapata Chardonnay (Argentina), Saddleback Pinot Blanc (California), WillaKenzie Pinot Blanc (Oregon) and the Fumé Blancs of Staton Hills (Washington), Ferrari Carano, De Loach, Byron, and Murphy-Goode (California).

OLD WORLD
You may also wish to try a Puligny-Montrachet, such as those of Chartron and Leflaive, or a Chassagne-Montrachet from Champy.

Vin de Pays Grand Ardèche Chardonnay of Louis Latour is an affordable alternative.

ALTERNATIVES
For something different, try a Château Malfourat Monbazillac Cuvée Prestige or experiment with other sweet wines, such as "vendange tardive," late harvest and ice wines. For a light and sparkling sweet wine, try Soljans "Fusion" Muscat.

Thailand

HOR MOK
Steamed Curry Fish Custard

This is a spicy custard with pieces of fish buried inside. Traditionally, it is served in pretty cups made of banana leaves. These are quite easily made if banana leaves are available. Cut the leaves into 6-inch (15-cm) squares. Fold 1½ inches (4 cm) of the adjacent sides of the leaf upward to make two sides of an open box. Use a staple to hold the corner in place. Do the same for the other sides and corners. An alternative to banana leaf cups is to use small soufflé bowls.

10½ oz (300 g) white fish fillets
3 cups (675 ml) coconut milk
½ cup (110 ml) red curry paste (see page 114)
4 eggs
3 kaffir lime leaves, finely shredded
2 tbsp fish sauce (nam pla)
8 tbsp flour
1 cup Thai basil leaves
1 red chili, finely shredded

Cut the fish fillet into ½-inch (1½-cm) cubes. Separate the egg yolks from the whites.

Mix the red curry paste, 2 cups of the coconut milk, and the fish sauce. Stir in the flour, mixing very well, then include the egg yolks and two-thirds of the shredded kaffir lime leaves.

Line the banana leaf cups or soufflé bowls with the Thai basil leaves. Divide the fish among the cups and then pour in the curry mixture.

Prepare a steamer or a large wok for steaming. If you are using a wok, place a cake tin or steaming stand in the wok to support the heat-proof serving dish. Pour in enough water to bring the water level to 2 inches (5 cm) beneath the top of the cake tin or stand.

Place the cups on a tray that will fit into the steamer. Bring the water to a boil. Place the tray of filled cups into the steamer. Cover and steam over high heat for 15 minutes.

While the custard is cooking, prepare the topping by mixing the remaining 1 cup of coconut milk, 2 tablespoons flour, and the egg whites. Heat this over low heat without bringing to a boil.

When the cups of custard are firm but still moist, spoon the topping on each serving and garnish with the sliced chili and kaffir lime leaves. Steam for another minute and serve.

The combination of sprightliness coming from the kaffir lime leaves and the rounder, richer flavors of the coconut milk calls for a wine with the same blend of crisp acidity and soft, rounded flavor.

OLD WORLD
Julian Chivite Gran Feudo Rosé from the Navarra in Spain. Another good partner is Castello della Sala Cervaro (a Chardonnay and Grechetto blend) is like a bouquet of wildflowers, with a lemony finesse.

NEW WORLD & OLD WORLD
Any good blend that features Chardonnay. Also look for Semillion-Sauvignon blends from Australia. Reliable brands include de Bortoli's Gulf Station, Cape Mentelle, Cullens, and Angoves. Interesting blended Italian whites include the wonderfully versatile Vintage Tunina from Jermann, Terre Alte from Livio Felluga, Braide Alte from Livon, and Lis from Lis Neris.

ALTERNATIVES
Sauvignon Blanc from the fruity to the grassy can be served. Try Merry Edwards, Cakebread, Mondavi (California), Monkey Bay, Oyster Bay, Kim Crawford, Seresin and State Landt (New Zealand), or any Sancerre (France). Favorites include Pascal Jolivet, Natter, Gitton, Cotat, Mellot, and Nozat.

Fiery or Sweet Flavors

The hallmark of the recipes in this section is spicy hotness or rich sweetness. The primary seasonings are hot chilies, cloves, sugar, palm sugar, and mustard seeds. Pastes and sauces include chili paste, hot curry paste, Hoisin sauce, kechap manis, mirin, sweet and sour sauce, sweet soy sauce, chutney, and sauces made from fresh or dried fruit.

You can make a successful match with any of the light to medium-sweet wines in Category 4 or, in the case of very sweet dishes, wines from Category 5. The rich flavor of these wines enfolds and subdues the spicy element in the food. For those who enjoy a fiery tingle on the palate, we suggest matching demi-sec sparkling wine or even well-chilled fruity reds from Category 2.

India
GOAN VINDALOO
Meat Curry

The Portuguese, who colonized the tiny region of Goa (known as the Pearl of the Orient) for hundreds of years, left their mark on its cuisine in the form of a propensity for tomatoes, pork, garlic, and the use of red wine in cooking. The Portuguese also introduced chilies to the region, so it should come as no surprise that Goa produces the most famous of hot curries: Vindaloo.

1 lb (500 g) lean pork
$^1/_4$ cup (60 ml) oil
2 stalks curry leaves
1 cup (225 ml) water
1 large onion, sliced
1 tsp salt

Spice paste
$^1/_2$ tsp mustard seeds, ground
2 tsp ground cumin
3 tsp ground black pepper
1 tbsp ground cinnamon
4 cardamoms, crushed
3 tbsp chili powder
$^1/_2$ cup (60 ml) vinegar
3 onions, sliced and fried
4 cloves garlic
2-inch (5-cm) piece of ginger

Cut the pork up into $1^1/_2$-inch (3-cm) cubes. Grind all the ingredients for the spice paste together in a food processor until smooth.

Heat the oil in a deep pan and fry the paste until the oil rises to the surface. Add the pork to the paste and sauté continuously for 5 minutes until the meat is coated. Add the curry leaves and 1 cup of water to the pan and cover.

Simmer the meat for 45 minutes, stirring occasionally to prevent the mixture from sticking. Remove the lid, add the sliced onions, and salt to taste. Continue cooking till the gravy is thick.

The fiery gravy of this dish calls for a well-balanced and elegant sweet white wine from Category 5 wines. It does not matter whether the wine is complex, with many layers of flavor, or just offers straightforward grapey or raisin-like sensations. We are looking for sweetness and coolness in temperature to temper the fiery chili.

OLD WORLD
Serve a well-made Recioto di Soave. This wine's crisp acidity highlights the spices and cleanses the palate, while its well-balanced sweetness interacts with the chilies to create an attractively soft, rounded sensation. Good producers include Coffele, Gini, Pieropan, Bolla, Vicentini, and Ca' Rugate. Muscat de Beaumes-de-Venise, Muscat de Rivesaltes, Muscat de Frontignan, Muscat de Lunel, Muscat de Miravel, and Muscat du Cap Corse (all from France) are other interesting matches. You can also confidently match sweet Greek wines, such as those of Samos or the Tsantali Mavrodaphne, with this dish.

NEW WORLD
Muscats are our New World favorites for this dish. Choose from Texas Hills Vineyard Orange Moscato, Quady "Essensia" California Orange Muscat, or Morris Wines Cellar Release Liqueur Muscat (Australia). Nothing generates conversation like the Indonesian Hatten Estate's Pino De Bali.

ALTERNATIVES
You might like to try a well-chilled rosé. Try a Regaleali Rosato from Sicily, Italy; a Chivite Gran Feudo Rosado from Navarra, Spain; a La Vieille Ferme Rhône Valley Rosé from France; a Bonny Doon Vin Gris de Cigare from California, or a Charles Melton Barossa Valley Rosé from Australia.

Thailand

KAENG KHAO WAN
Chicken in Green Curry

In Thailand, red curries are medium hot while green curries are much hotter. Green curries are traditionally accompanied with rice noodles, although these curries are now commonly served with rice.

Green curry paste
6 green chilies
2 tbsp chopped shallots
1 tbsp chopped garlic
2 stalks lemongrass
1 tbsp shrimp paste
1 tbsp chopped galangal (lengkuas)
1 tsp cumin seeds
1 tsp coriander seeds
1 tsp minced kaffir lime (limau purut) or lemon zest
1 tsp salt

Cut off the white stem of the lemongrass and discard the leaves. Trim off the root and slice the stem into rounds. Wash the chilies under cold running water and remove their stems. Slit open the chilies and discard the seeds.

Blend the chilies and all the other ingredients in a food processor to make a smooth paste, adding water a little at a time if necessary. The paste can be frozen and used as required.

1$^1/_2$ lbs (750 g) chicken breasts
3 cups (675 ml) coconut milk
2 tbsp green curry paste
4 kaffir lime leaves
1 eggplant, diced
2 tbsp fish sauce (nam pla)
1 green chili, sliced and deseeded
4 fresh sweet Thai basil leaves (horapha)

Slice the chicken breasts into 1 x 2 inch (2$^1/_2$ x 5 cm) strips. Boil the eggplant till soft. Drain and set aside.

Put half a cup of the coconut milk in a large saucepan and bring to a boil. Reduce the heat and simmer. Add 2 tablespoons of the green curry paste and the kaffir lime leaves, and then increase the heat. Stir from time to time until a thick curry is obtained.

Add the chicken and cook for 2 minutes. Stir in the remaining coconut milk, the eggplant, and the fish sauce. Simmer uncovered for 10 minutes. Taste for seasoning and garnish with the fresh sweet basil and chili. Serve with steamed rice.

A lightly sweet wine will calm the chili and also echo the texture of the coconut, although any of the sweeter wines in Category 5 will work too.

OLD WORLD
Pick a Côteaux du Layon from Clos Baudoin or Château Haut Bernasse's Monbazillac. A light and lively Moscato d'Asti also works well with this spicy dish as it adds an extra dimension of pleasure with its fresh, grapey fragrance. From Austria, Nekowitsch Schilfwein "The Red One" makes a good red wine liaison while the excellently balanced, pineapple-tart flavored Shuckert Grüner Veltliner is our white choice. Other Austrian or German wines (Auslese or sweeter) can work their magic here too.

NEW WORLD
Try wines like Concha Y Toro's Late Harvest Sauvignon Blanc (Chile) and Montana's Late Harvest Selection (New Zealand).

ALTERNATIVES
From the New World, try the Chardonnays of Sileni Estate, Church Road, Esk Valley, Matariki, and Beach House, all from New Zealand. Their rounded nature mirrors the texture of the dish, and the toasty vanilla notes blend with the coconut-milk flavors of the curry.

Why not try French Vin de Pays Chardonnays? Spain's Navarra region offers an unoaked Grenache red wine from Guelbenzu that is fruity and well structured. Its crisp acidity and supple body will brighten the flavors of this dish.

Sri Lanka

ELOLU CURRY
Vegetable Curry

Sri Lanka is a fig-shaped island located off the southeast tip of the Indian subcontinent. The Portuguese, who dominated the island in the sixteenth and seventeenth centuries, and the Dutch, who held sway in the seventeenth and eighteenth centuries, left a liking for sweets and the liberal use of chili spice. Sri Lankan curry seasonings are generally roasted before blending, which adds a darker color and distinctive smoky character. Grated coconut and coconut milk are used freely in the cuisine.

This versatile recipe is also suitable for any leafy vegetable, eggplant, and okra, or a combination of vegetables.

10 oz (300 g) leeks
1 tsp curry powder
6 red onions, sliced
1 sprig curry leaves
$^1/_4$ tsp dill seeds
$^1/_4$ tsp saffron
1 cup coconut cream
3 tsp chili powder
1 tsp ground cumin
3 green chilies, sliced
3 tbsp oil

Heat a pan without oil and dry roast the curry powder. Stir continuously for about 3 minutes, making sure it does not burn. Set aside.

Clean and cut the leeks into half-inch ($2^1/_4$-cm) pieces. Rinse and set aside. Heat the oil and stir fry the leeks. Remove the leeks when they begin to soften. Using the oil left in the pan, fry the sliced red onions, curry leaves, and dill seeds. Add the saffron. When the onions turn brown, add the leeks, coconut cream, chili powder, cumin powder, and chilies.

Cover and cook for about 15 minutes. When the curry takes on an oily sheen, adjust for salt, sprinkle with the roasted curry powder, and serve with steamed rice.

The effervescence of a lightly sweet sparkling wine will lift the hefty flavors of the curry. You will find such wines in Category 4. Sweet wines from Category 5 also have a place here, as do the light reds from Category 2.

OLD WORLD
A Prosecco Extra Dry will give an effervescent tingle, while its light sweetness will calm the chili heat. There are many fine producers of this Italian wine, among them Villa Sandi, Bisol, and Carpenè Malvolti. Also the Crémant d' Alsace from Josmeyer, Lucien Albrecht, and Domaine Pierre Sparr are good choices. The creamy quality of the mousse softly cleanses the palate and echoes the texture of the dish. Sweeter wines also work well.

NEW WORLD
The Late Harvest or botrytised wines of Vina Undurraga (Chile), De Bortoli (Australia), and De Loach Gewürztraminer (California), as well as the lighter style Peju "Provence" blend (California), are favorites.

ALTERNATIVES
Try a light and lively red or rosé, such as Montepulciano d'Abruzzo Cerasuolo (Italy) or a simple Beaujolais (France). Good producers for this latter wine include Georges Duboeuf, Pierre Marie Chermette, Henry Fessy, and Chateau des Jacques.

China

SZECHUAN CHICKEN WITH DRIED CHILIES

Szechuan is the largest province in China. Its cuisine is noted for being hot, spicy, and strongly flavored, with chili, pungent garlic, and spring onions playing important roles. Chili peppers may have arrived in this region along with the Indian Buddhist missionaries who traveled the Silk Route. Another theory suggests that Portuguese and Spanish sailors traded chili with merchants at Chinese seaports.

1 lb (500 g) chicken breasts, deboned and skinned
2 tsp sherry
$1/2$ tsp sesame oil
1 tsp light soy sauce
1 tsp dark soy sauce
10 dried chilies
2 stalks scallions (spring onions)
A handful of cashew nuts
9 tbsp oil
8 slices ginger
2 cloves of garlic, sliced
1 tsp Szechuan pepper
$1/4$ tsp salt
1 tbsp sugar

Cut the chicken into 1-inch ($2^1/_2$-cm) cubes and marinate in the sherry, sesame oil, and the light and dark soy sauces. Slit the chilies and discard the seeds. Remove the green tops of the scallions and slice the white bulb into 1-inch ($2^1/_2$-cm) lengths.

Heat 6 tablespoons of oil in a frying pan till it is smoking. Stir fry the chicken pieces till they are golden brown. Drain and set aside. Heat the remaining 3 tablespoons oil and fry the ginger and garlic until they turn golden. Add the chilies and Szechuan pepper. Stir fry, making sure that the chilies do not burn. Include the chicken, cashew nuts, and the scallions. Stir, then season with salt and sugar to taste. Remove and serve with steamed rice.

The combination of dried chilies with garlic, sesame oil, and soy sauce creates a powerful flavor, so it's a good idea to choose a wine with personality as well as a touch of sweetness. The sweetness in any Category 5 wine provides a soothing backdrop for the hotness of the Szechuan pepper and dried chilies.

OLD WORLD
Try a Gewürztraminer Alsace Sélection de Grains Nobles, or an Austrian or German beerenauslese. Chenin Blanc-based, lightly sweet Vouvray (moelleux or demi-sec) wines work well here too. Favorite producers of this latter wine are Jean-Pierre Laisenent, Domaine Bourillon d'Orléans, Domaine Georges Brunet, and Marc Bredif. The style of these wines enfolds the spices and hot sensations, creating interesting textural matches or contrasts with the food.

NEW WORLD
A Texas winery, Fall Creek, stands out for its soft, lightly sweet Chenin Blanc. Also fragrant, off-dry Muscat works well. Try one from Messina-Hof, also from Texas, or one from the Golan Heights Yarden winery in Israel.

ALTERNATIVES
A well-chilled, medium-priced Australian red, such as Jacob's Creek Grenache or Shiraz, Penfolds' Rawson's Retreat Shiraz or Cabernet, or Nottage Hill Merlot, also has the touch of residual sweetness to take on the chili.

Singapore / Malaysia

FISH-HEAD CURRY

Long a favorite in Malaysia and Singapore, fish-head curry is now turning up on restaurant menus in New York, Boston, and other cosmopolitan cities.

This version retains its original Malay flavor by including a dab of pungent shrimp paste, a key ingredient of many Malay dishes. Known as belacan (pronounced blah-charn), it consists of tiny shrimp cured in salt, formed into a small brick and sun-dried. It is also available in a bottled version. A little belacan goes a long, long way, so use it sparingly to enhance the flavor of meats, fish, and seafood. Firm white fish (whole or filleted), shrimp, or lobster may be substituted for the fish head in this recipe.

1 large fish head, about 1 1/2 lb (700 g)
1/2 tsp salt
3 tbsp tamarind pulp
3 cups water
2 stalks lemongrass (optional)
2 tbsp oil
2 tbsp sugar
4 okra (lady fingers)
2 tomatoes

Spice paste
5 slices galangal (lengkuas)
1 tbsp turmeric powder
30 shallots
2 tsp shrimp paste (belacan)
4 red chilies
3 dried chilies, soaked till soft
5 candlenuts (buah keras) or 10 macadamia nuts

Rub the fish head with the salt. Put the tamarind pulp in 3 cups of hot water and mash the pulp with the back of a spoon until the pulp disintegrates. Strain and retain the liquid. Trim off the roots of the lemongrass, keeping the white stems and leaves intact.

Blend the spice paste ingredients in a food processor, adding water a teaspoon at a time if necessary, until a smooth paste is obtained.

Heat 2 tablespoons of oil in a wok or pan and fry the paste for about 5 minutes until it is fragrant. Add the tamarind liquid, lemongrass, and sugar and bring to a boil. Meanwhile, trim off the tops of the okra and cut the tomatoes into quarters. Add the fish to the boiling liquid and simmer for 5 minutes. Put in the okra and tomatoes and simmer for a further 7 minutes or until the fish is cooked. Add more water if necessary.

This is a dish that combines many flavors and textures. We suggest that you choose a wine that is not too dry and is supple, fragrant, and has zippy acidity. But beware: a wine that is too sweet makes too much of a contrast, and the sourness of the dish may be overly accentuated.

OLD WORLD
Vouvray Demi-Sec is an excellent partner. Its sweetness combines with the chili to create a lush, round sensation in the mouth. Its crisp flavor also sets off the candlenuts. Reliable producers include Vincent Raimbault, François Chidaine, and Domaine Huet L'Echansonne.

NEW WORLD
Dry or off-dry South African Chenin Blancs from De Trafford, Stellenbosch Vineyards, Rudera, and Villiera are worth seeking out.

ALTERNATIVES
Chili lovers might like to experience the tingling sensation on the palate that occurs when very, very cold demi-sec sparkling wine combines with chili heat. The best-known Spanish Cava brands are Freixenet and Codorníu.

German Sekt, such as those from Henkell & Sohnlein or Kurpfalz Sektkellerei, or New World sparklers, such as California's Schramsberg Demi-Sec, Australia's fruity Rumball Sparkling Shiraz, and New Zealand's Cellier le Brun Brut (whose fruity aromatics disguise the dry nature of the wine) are engaging alternatives.

In Asia, a popular way of handling sweet wines that are intended to accompany a meal is to add several ice cubes to each glass. This treatment tones down the richly sweet character of the wine.

Singapore

PEPPER CRAB

In Singapore, crab may be cooked over a barbeque or in a bean sauce, stir fried with chili, steamed with garlic, or baked with salt. However, the most popular versions are chili crab and pepper crab. Connoisseurs are divided as to which is better. Mud crabs or swimmer crabs may be used in this recipe.

2 lbs (1 kg) crabs
6 tbsp black peppercorns
3 tbsp butter
2 Spanish onions, shredded
2 tsp minced garlic
2 tbsp minced shallots
$^1/_2$ cup (115 ml) chicken stock
2 tbsp light soy sauce
2 tsp dark soy sauce
2 tsp sugar
2 stalks leaf cilantro (coriander leaves), torn into sprigs

Crush the peppercorns in a blender or with a mortar and pestle. Set aside.

To clean the crabs, use a knife to pry off the flap on the underside. Remove the shell by putting your thumb on the top and fingers on the front, lifting the shell upward. Clear away the innards revealed under the shell. Chop the crabs into pieces and clean thoroughly under running water.

Heat the butter in a large frying pan or wok. Fry the crushed peppercorns, shredded onions, garlic, and shallots. When the onions are transparent, add the chicken stock, both the light and dark soy sauces, and the sugar. Mix well, turn up the heat, and then add the crab.

Cook the crab over medium heat, stirring occasionally. The crabs are done when the shells turn red (about 5 minutes). Garnish with the leaf cilantro and serve.

A medium-bodied, fruity red or rosé is an excellent backdrop for the peppercorns and butter that are the predominant ingredients of this dish. There are many Category 2 and Category 4 wines to choose from.

OLD WORLD
A sparkling rosé is a stylish choice. Its effervescence creates a tingling sensation on the palate, and its color pleases the eye. Try one from Italy's Franciacorta area. The producers in this zone are noted for maintaining very high quality standards, so you will be safe with any Franciacorta. However, we particularly like the lightly toasted almondy Contaldi Castaldi Franciacorta Rosé.

Côtes de Provence rosés, such as Domaine Gavoty, Domaine des Aspras, and Domaine de la Sauveuse make good liaisons. Try also La Baume Syrah Rosé, and Vin de Pays d'Oc.

NEW WORLD
Excellent producers of attractive New World pink wines include Badger Mountain (Washington); Beringer Nouveau or Mumm Napa (California); Lindemans Bin 35 (Australia); Lindauer NV (New Zealand); and Santa Rita Cabernet Sauvignon Rosé (Chile).

ALTERNATIVES
Red wines made from ripe fruit and with somewhat higher alcohol levels and some sweetness in them work well here. Try Pinot Noirs and Zinfandels from any New World country. Brown Brothers Tarrango (Australia), made from an unusual grape variety, has succulent red-berry flavors and would make a very interesting match.

India

SWEET PILAU

The Persian word *pilaou* is probably derived from the Turkish *pilav*: both words mean boiled rice. Alternative spellings are *pilaff, pilaf, pilau,* and "*pilaw.*" English writers began mentioning this dish in the seventeenth century, when the British Empire spread through the Middle East into India.

1 lb (500 g) basmati rice
$^1/_2$ cup (100 g) ghee
$^1/_2$ cup raisins
$^1/_2$ cup (100 g) almonds, blanched
$^1/_2$ cup (110 g) pistachios, blanched
4 cardamoms
6 cloves
5-cm stick cinnamon
$^1/_2$ tsp mace powder
$^1/_2$ tsp saffron or turmeric powder
$^1/_4$ tsp salt
$^1/_2$ cup (100 g) sugar
3 cups (675 ml) water
4 tbsp melted ghee
Rose water

Wash the rice in water and drain. Repeat till the water runs clear. Put 3 cups of water in a saucepan and bring to a boil.

Heat half a cup of ghee in a pan and sauté the raisins, almonds, and pistachios until they turn light brown. Remove the raisins and nuts, leaving behind the ghee.

Add the rice to the pan and lightly brown over low heat. Add the cardamoms, cloves, cinnamon, mace, saffron, salt, sugar, and the 3 cups of boiling water. Bring the mixture to a boil over high heat and cook for a further 5 minutes, then lower the heat and cover until done. This will take about 20 minutes; the rice will have fluffed up, and all the liquid will have evaporated. Pour in the melted ghee, stir gently, and add the nuts and raisins. Sprinkle with rose water.

Note: This pilau can be served on its own. However, if you wish to have it with raan, you should use the wine suggestions for the meat dish.

Choose a well-balanced wine that is sweet enough to stand up to the almonds, raisins, and sugar in this recipe. Most Category 5 wines will fit the bill.

OLD WORLD
A favorite is Passito di Pantelleria Bukkuram from Marco De Bartoli in Sicily, which tastes of candied fruit and dried apricot, with a sprinkling of nutmeg and cinnamon. Another fine example from Sicily is Ben Ryé from Donnafugata. Alois Kracher (Austria) and Alain Brumont (France) also offer excellent wines befitting this dish.

NEW WORLD
Try Asara Noble Late Harvest (South Africa) and well-chilled ice wines from Jackson Triggs (Canada).

ALTERNATIVES
Richly textured sweet wines of France: the nutty, caramel-like Macvin du Jura (white, red, or rosé) has a particular affinity to the flavors of this dish. A favorite Macvin is from Domaine de la Pinte. The rich, sweet character and occasionally rancio taste of Pineau de Charente (white or rosé) also matches this regal dish. You may also wish to experiment with New World sherry-styled wine.

Japan

SHABU SHABU

Shabu Shabu is the onomatopoeic name for food swished around in a simmering broth. This one-pot dish, or *nabemono* in Japanese, is hearty winter fare where all diners take part in cooking ingredients at the table. Some nabemono feature wild boar or horse. This Shabu Shabu uses beef and vegetables, although you can substitute lamb loin for the beef. Usually, Shabu Shabu slices are thinner than Sukiyaki slices and should measure about 8 x 3 inches (20 x 8 cm). Both are available in Japanese supermarkets.

1 1/4 lbs (600 g) rump or sirloin steak, cut into paper-thin slices
1/4 head Chinese cabbage
5 oz (150 g) spinach
2 carrots
8 shitake mushrooms
2 leeks
9 oz (300 g) tofu
6 cups (1 1/4 liters) vegetable stock
Ponzu sauce
1 scallion (spring onion), finely chopped

Cut the tofu and vegetables into bite-sized pieces. If you are using dried mushrooms, you will need to hydrate them in a bowl of boiling water for about 10 minutes, then squeeze them dry, and trim off the stems.

Arrange all the ingredients, including the steak and tofu, on a platter. Pour the Ponzu sauce into small, individual dipping dishes, and add a sprinkle of chopped scallions.

To cook and serve, put a large flame-proof casserole or clay pot on a burner in the center of the table and fill the pot two-thirds full with the vegetable stock. When the stock is simmering, diners cook their food in it by picking up the beef and vegetables with chopsticks and swishing each piece in the stock for a few seconds until it is done to their liking. Once cooked, the morsels should be dipped in Ponzu sauce and consumed with rice. Add more stock as it boils off.

Ponzu sauce is available in Asian supermarkets.

The savory, sweet, and lemony taste of this dish comes from the Ponzu dipping sauce. Do match Shabu Shabu with a full-blown sweet wine or any wine from Category 5.

OLD WORLD
We recommend two excellent sweet wines from Italy. Fattoria Zerbina's Albana di Romagna Arrocco Passito has a rich, warming fragrance and the flavor of very ripe pears and vibrant tangerine zest, leaving the palate refreshingly clean. Castello della Sala's Muffato della Sala tastes of pineapple and acacia honey, and its fresh style helps to cleanse the palate. Well-chilled Inniskillin Ice Wine Gold Oak Aged (Canada) works well, as does the Austrian Eiswein of Hopler.

Hungarian Tokaji has an oily richness that merges well with the texture of the sticky rice. The fortified sweet red wines of Banyuls in France, from producers such as Gauby Domaine du Mas Blanc and Domaine des Templiers are other possibilities for textural liaison. The adventurous might try a Pedro Ximénez Sherry or Malaga, which display a rich consistency and wonderful raisiny sweetness.

NEW WORLD
You will find U.S. wines such as Bonny Doon's Muscat Vin de Glaciere (California), Fiori delle Stelle Vidal Ice Wine (New York), and Silvan Ridge Early Muscat (Oregon) to be just as ideal as those from Europe.

Indonesia

AYAM PANGGANG PEDAS
Spicy Grilled Chicken

This Indonesian-style grilled chicken is quick and easy to make and will certainly give a lift to any barbeque menu.

3 lbs (1 $^1/_2$ kg) chicken pieces
Lime wedges
Kaffir lime leaves (daun limau purut)

Marinade
2 tsp salt
3 tsp black pepper
3 tsp chili powder
1 tsp ground coriander
2 tbsp onion, sliced
1 tbsp chopped garlic
2 tbsp dark soy sauce
3 tsp sugar
2 tbsp lime or lemon juice
2 tbsp oil

Score the skin and flesh of the chicken. Combine all the other ingredients to make a marinade and rub it all over the chicken pieces. Cover and refrigerate for 2 hours to chill.

Preheat a grill or a coal barbeque. When it is hot, cook the chicken pieces, using any leftover marinade for basting. Ensure that you do not char the chicken, but cook it until the skin is golden brown. Test for doneness by piercing a thigh with a knife. If the juice runs clear, the chicken is ready.

Squeeze some lime juice over the chicken and serve with additional wedges of lime and finely shredded kaffir lime leaves.

This chicken dish is savory, sweet, spicy, nutty, and smoky – with a citrus note as well! With so many dimensions of taste, it offers great latitude for wine matching. You could serve a Chardonnay with mineral or tropical fruit flavors such as a Camelot Highlands from Santa Barbara. A soft, ripe, and fruity Merlot like Toasted Head Merlot from California would work well too, as does a sweet wine.

OLD WORLD
Port on ice – we liked Quinto do Vesuvio. For the adventurous, try Massandra Muskabel Rosé (Ukraine).

NEW WORLD
The light sweetness of the excellently balanced Hogue Cellars (Washington) Johannisberg Riesling provides sufficient body to take on the various flavors and textures of the dish. Try also the Trinchero Estate White Zinfandel (California) or the Jacob's Creek Sparkling Rosé (Australia), which refresh the palate with every sip.

If you prefer full-on sweetness, Anakena Late Harvest (Chile) is a good match.

ALTERNATIVES
Try any light-bodied red wine from Category 2.

Singapore / Malaysia
DEVIL CURRY

This Eurasian stew, also called Curry Debal, is a legacy of the Portuguese who settled in Malaysia and who cooked their version of curry during festive seasons, especially at Christmas. Traditionally, this dish is fiery hot. Some say Devil Curry is not Devil Curry until your mouth burns and sweat pours off your brow, so adjust the chili heat according to your taste.

3 lbs (1$\frac{1}{2}$ kg) chicken pieces
3 oz (100 g) roasted pork, sliced
2 pork sausages, cut in half
2 potatoes, boiled and cut into wedges
1 carrot, boiled and cut into wedges
2 tomatoes, in quarter wedges
3 green chilies
2 red chilies
6 tbsp oil
$\frac{1}{4}$ tsp salt
1 tsp chili powder
2 tbsp turmeric powder
2 tbsp mustard
4 tbsp vinegar
$\frac{1}{4}$ tsp sugar
Lemon juice
1 cucumber, cored and cut into large pieces

Spice ingredients
10 red chilies, seeds removed
10 dried red chilies, seeds removed
2 large onions
12 shallots
7 cloves garlic
1-inch (2$\frac{1}{2}$-cm) piece of ginger
1 candlenut

Grind the spice ingredients into a fine paste in a food processor. Set aside. Mix the chili powder and turmeric powder with a little water to form a smooth paste. Set aside.

Heat the oil in a wok and fry the spice paste for 10 minutes or until fragrant. Add the chicken and the salt, and fry over high heat for a few minutes. Add the chili and tumeric paste. Stir well, add a little water, and continue to cook over low heat.

When the chicken is just about cooked through, add the pork, sausage, potato, carrot, tomato, green and red chilies, mustard, vinegar, and sugar. Stir and simmer for another 10 minutes. Season with lemon juice and garnish with cucumber pieces. Serve with steamed rice.

The fire in this dish is best quelled by a sweet wine.

OLD WORLD
Muscat de Beaumes de Venise (Domain de Durban or Jaboulet), Domaine Weinbach Riesling Schlossberg (Alsace, France), and dessert wines of Artinger, Reinisch, Umathum, and Mantlerhof (Austria) all work well.

NEW WORLD
Good matches are botrytised and sweet wines: Brown Brothers Patricia, Noble One (Australia), Sileni Pourriture Noble (New Zealand), Ravenswood Late Harvest Gewürztraminer Dolce, and Quady (all from California).

ALTERNATIVES
The effervescence in a sparkling wine accentuates the spiciness of the dish. Try Freixenet Cava (Spain), Henriot (France), and Taltarni Brut Taché (Australia). We suggest trying other sparkling rosés too. Category 1 wines with lemony-tart characters cleanse the palate, so they might be served too.

ASIAN MENUS

We have devised a number of menus based on the fifty recipes in this book to help you impress guests with your skill at matching wines with home-cooked Asian meals. These menus are designed for communal meals, with all the dishes served at the same time, in the Asian tradition. Generally speaking, for these menus we suggest that you have both a red (or rosé) and a white wine on the table. We also urge you to have a crisp, sweet wine as well. Sip the appropriate wines as you taste the various foods.

Our wine suggestions enable you to cross flavor and recipe boundaries without resorting to a specific wine for each course.

Although we have listed a specific wine for each dish, this does not mean that you must serve or sip only the prescribed wine. Traditionally, white wines never follow red wines at a dinner or a tasting. With communal dining this "rule" can be broken. We would advise that after tasting a red, you take a mouthful of food to reinstate your palate before going back to a white wine. While a high-tannin red (Category 6) would be an excellent choice with certain dishes when they are served Western-style, such wines do not easily fit within the context of an Asian communal meal. We therefore suggest that a softer red, such as those listed in Category 3, be substituted since this type of wine will be able to make liaisons with a wider variety of flavors. One of the pleasures of communal dining with wine is that it is possible to explore your own taste preferences with greater freedom.

Communal Asian Meals

The Spicy Palate
Thai Fish Cakes (fresh and herbal)
Udang Pantung Kuning (savory and rich)
Rogan Josh (savory and rich)
Vegetable Curry (fiery and sweet)
Sweet Pilau (fiery and sweet)

Crisp wines and dry, aromatic wines from Category 1 for the Thai Fish Cakes.
Fruity soft-tannin reds from Category 3 for Udang Patung Kuning and
Rogan Josh.
Lightly sweet to medium-sweet wines (medium-dry, off-dry) from Category 4
for the Vegetable Curry and Sweet Pilau.

Chinese Home-style Meal
Cantonese Steamed Snapper (fresh and herbal)
Braised Mushrooms and Mustard Greens (savory and rich)
Steamed Chicken with Ham (mildly spicy and light smoky)
Caramelized Shrimp (fresh and herbal)
Soup: Although wine is not usually drunk with soup, no Chinese meal is
complete without it. You could make an authentic Chinese-style soup by
adding leafy vegetables or cubed potatoes and carrots to a rich chicken stock.
Dessert: Sliced fruits may be served as dessert, as they are in Chinese restaurants.

Crisp wines and dry, aromatic wines from Category 1 for the seafood and chicken.
Fruity soft-tannin reds from Category 3 for the mushroom dish.

Asian Brunch

Mango Salad (mildly spicy and light smoky)

Sambal Babi (mildly spicy and light smoky)

Kai Yang (spicy and smoky)

Laksa Lemak (spicy and smoky)

Juicy white wines, medium rosé wines, and light red wines from Category 2 or aromatic wines from Category 1 for the Mango Salad and Sambal Babi. Woody white wines and fruity soft-tannin red wines from Category 3 for the Kai Yang and Laksa Lemak.

Cold Asian Picnic

Laap (fresh and herbal)

Squid Salad (fresh and herbal)

Mango Salad (mildly spicy and light smoky)

Ayam Panggang Pedas (fiery and sweet)

Tandoori Chicken (spicy and smoky)

Imperial-style Grilled Spareribs (spicy and smoky)

Crisp wines and dry, aromatic wines from Category 1 for the Laap and squid. Well-chilled fruity reds from Category 2 for the Mango Salad and Spicy Grilled Chicken.

Woody white wines and fruity soft-tannin red wines from Category 3 for the Tandoori Chicken and spareribs.

Pan-Asian Banquet served Western Style

This group of recipes is designed in the style of a Western meal and is, therefore, served in courses. Simply choose appropriate wines for each course according to suggestions given with the recipes. The following menu would feature wines from Category 1, Category 2, Category 5, and Category 6 according to the flavors of the dish.

Starters
Spiced Mussels (fresh and herbal)
Laap (fresh and herbal)

Entrée
Gado Gado (spicy and smoky)

Fish Course
Meen Varuval (mildly spicy and light smoky)
Pepper Crab (fiery and sweet)

Main Course
Goan Vindaloo (fiery and sweet)
Vegetable Curry (fiery and sweet)
Raan (savory and rich)
Sweet Pilau (fiery and sweet)

Dessert
Chilled Longan in Lime Syrup
Simply open a can of longan and serve chilled with a squeeze of lime.

Asian Finger Foods for Wine Tasting

The group of recipes is a specially chosen collection of Asian finger foods for wine tasting. Each dish represents a different flavor as well as the cusine from particular Asian countries.

Goi Cuon (fresh and herbal)
Meen Varuval (mildly spicy and light smoky)
Imperial-style Grilled Spareribs (spicy and smoky)
Yakitori (savory and rich)
Szechuan Chicken with Dried Chilies (fiery and sweet)

Asian Restaurant Fare

This section provides general guidelines for matching wine with typical Asian restaurant offerings.

Dim Sum or Yum Cha

Yum cha literally means "to drink tea." Weary travelers on the Silk Road would refresh themselves at the teahouses alongside farmers from nearby rural communities who ended their hard day's work with a sip of tea. Teahouses began serving small food dishes (dim sum) to complement the tea. These bite-sized morsels offer a wonderful variety of textures and flavors: steamed, deep-fried, and braised dishes, and sweet, sour, and hot. Spices are mild, and chili dipping sauce is served alongside. Thus, yum cha has come to mean a snack of dim sum and tea, but that, of course, does not preclude the enjoyment of wine with the food.

A general wine to go with the wide variety of steamed, fried, and braised dim sum is Pinot Gris or Pinot Grigio (Category 2).

Also try lightly sweet wines with the zest and aromas of a fruit basket from Category 4. This is a category of wines that has been undervalued. We urge you to try a lightly sweet wine, such as a demi-sec Vouray, a Spätlese, or a Lambrusco, with dim sum.

Kaiseki Banquet

The Japanese kaiseki is an art form where a cornucopia of gastronomic treats made from fresh, seasonal ingredients is served with much pomp. Exquisite care is taken in selecting ingredients that are then prepared in ways that exalt their flavors and are presented on serving ware that is chosen to enhance the appearance and the seasonal theme of the meal. A banquet will include steamed, simmered, and grilled dishes and various courses, such as sashimi and sushi, tempura, grilled fish, steak, tofu, vegetables, soup, and rice. The wine chosen to accompany such a feast must be versatile.

A good general wine for the sushi, tempura, and grilled fish would be dry sparkling wine: Prosecco, Cava, or Clairette du Die. These wines have some tartness to cut through the oily fish and crispy fried food, and a lightly sweet taste enables the wine to match other dishes, including grills and soups. For the steak we suggest a Côtes du Rhône or Shiraz.

Also try lightly sweet wines form Category 4. These wines work surprisingly well, adding another dimension of texture and flavor. Combining a lightly sweet wine with savory foods opens the door to a new world of enjoyment.

For the adventurous, match the steak dish (which might be marinated or grilled) with a Rasteau or port from Category 7.

Chinese Banquet

A well-planned Chinese banquet will feature different tastes and textures. Firmness will be balanced by softness, smoothness by coarseness, crispness by stickiness, and juiciness by dryness.

Typically, a meal begins with a cold appetizer followed by a hot soup. A salty entrée (fried, roasted, or smoked poultry, such as Peking Duck) might be followed by another meat or seafood dish (pork, shrimp, or scallops). Then a meat course (like beefsteak or ribs) may precede a serving of crunchy stir-fried vegetables. A fish – deep-fried, braised, or steamed – is usually the last savory dish. Rice is eaten as a background to the various flavors of the banquet. Dessert will usually be a fruit or buns with a sweet filling, a sweet soup (served hot or cold), or red-bean pancakes.

Because the dishes are so diverse in cooking method, style, and taste, you will need three all-purpose wines: a versatile white (such as Pinot Blanc, Semillon, or an unoaked or lightly oaked Chardonnay); a rosé (such as Rosé d'Anjou, Tavel, or Rosé de Provence) from Category 2; and a flexible fruity red (Merlot, Pinot Noir, Cabernet Franc, or Nero D'Avola) from Category 3. If you wish to serve a different wine with each course, consider this:

Cold dish: A spumante or demi-sec sparkling wine

Soup: No wine

Fish: Semillon, Chenin Blanc, or unoaked Chardonnay

Fried, roasted, or smoked poultry: Pinot Noir or Rosé d'Anjou

Meat or seafood dishes: Pinot Noir or Rosé d'Anjou

Red Meat: Cabernet blends

Stir-fried seasonal vegetables: No wine

Dessert: No wine

Northern Indian Fare

Indian cuisine is as diverse as its number of states, each of which has its own cultural history and religious traditions. In general, Indian cuisine can be divided into the north, south, east, and west. Northern Indian cuisine is sweeter and less spicy than its southern counterparts. Over the centuries, northern Indian fare has been influenced by the Arians, Moghuls, and Greeks as well as by people from China, Portugal, and Britain through trade, conquest, and travel. The use of "softer" spices and creamy curries makes northern Indian food friendly for wine.

A typical meal would start with samosas or pakoras. Then all the other dishes – meat cooked in a tandoori oven, vegetable curry, lentils (dal), dry fish curry, and a mild curry (korma) – will be served with breads (naan, chappati, poori, paratha) and a selection of side dishes or pickles. The meal ends with a dessert, usually kulfi, which is an ice cream.

Start with a dry white wine (Chenin Blanc or a dry sparkler) from Category 1 and then move on to a woody white (a lightly oaked Chardonnay or Semillon) from Category 3, which will make a liaison with all the dishes. For those who prefer a red wine, a fruity soft-tannin New World blend or varietal (also from Category 3) should make a satisfying match with most of the dishes.

Indochinese Meal

The flavors and tastes of lime, chili, sweet creamy coconut, and basil characterize this selection of dishes from a typical Indochinese meal. You would start with a cold salad (pomelo, young mango, or laap) and then move on to a curry (red curry or green curry), side dishes (such as Hor Mok), and a vegetable

dish, all served together and accompanied by rice. The meal ends with dessert, which may be fruit, sweet soups, or a selection of coconut cream-based cakes.

A fruity Fumé Blanc with a hint of smoke would be the general wine to try, or you might choose a fruity red, such as a Ribera del Duero, Rosso di Montalcino, or a Rosso di Montepulciano. In essence, you want a wine from Category 3: creamy whites with a toasted vanilla aroma and soft-textured reds with hints of sweet red fruits.

Singapore-Malaysia-Indonesian

In the context of a Southeast Asian meal, all dishes are consumed at the same time, accompanied by steamed rice. A typical meal may comprise satay, a salad (Rojak or Gado Gado), a grilled-fish dish, a dry curry (Rendang), a wet curry, and a vegetable curry (Sayor Lodeh).

Because the dishes are sweet and chili hot, the wines have to be almost as sweet. The sweetness in the wines in Category 4 helps to lighten the effect of the spicy heat. If you insist on a red wine, choose one from the New World that has some residual sugar.

Also try Category 2 and Category 4 rosés, such as Bandol, Montepulciano d'Abruzzo Cerasuolo, Portuguese Rosé, or White Zinfandel. All these wines have a touch of fruity sweetness.

Wine Index

Bold numbers indicate wines listed with recipes.

SILENI

CELLAR SELECTION

MARLBOROUGH

SAUVIGNON BLANC

2005

WINE OF NEW ZEALAND

General Index

ACKNOWLEDGEMENTS

The authors wish to thank friends, family and colleagues for their help and support in the preparation of this book. In particular, Michael Benson, Greg Cannon, Edward Chew, Connie Clarkson, Jerry Comfort (Beringer) Claire Contamine (BIVB), Excaliber Trading, Ken & Akiko Freeman, Thierry Fritsch (CIVA), Anita & Eck Kheng Goh, Randall Grahm (Bonny Doone Vineyard), Susan Griswold, Bob Hall, Yohan Handoyo, Russell & Becky Hone, Ryan Hong, David Howell, Scott Kaeser, Prapai Kraisornkovit, Joy Lee, Malini Lee, Richard Lieu (California Wine Institute), Georgina Lim, Loo Hui Min (Singapore Exhibition Services), Gianni Masciarelli, Steve Messinger, Meena Mylvaganam, Radhika Ojha (Italian Trade Commission), Mikel Orbe (Embassy of Spain), Andy Peck, Connie Po, Alain Ponsard (SOPEXA), Jean-Marc Poullet, Carol Powers, Rita Scribner, Sileni Estate, Bertold Salomon, Keith & Gillian Soon, Dorothy Tan, Leon Tan, Madeleine Tan (SOPEXA), Tan Su Yen, Michael Thurner (Austrian Wine Marketing Board), Y. N. Tye, Daisuke Utagawa, Bill Vander Water, the Verma family, Debbie Whitehead, Yeo Khim Noy and the New Zealand Trade and Enterprise.

The stemware featured in this book are courtesy of Bottega del Vino Crystal.

Vineyard and winery images on pages 6, 9, 24, 31, 36, 37 are courtesy of the Austrian Wine Marketing Board, and those on pages 25, 30, 32 and 41 are by Edwin Soon. Remaining images by Ee Kay Gie.